T0316549

Cambridge Elements ≡

Elements in the Philosophy of Immanuel Kant
edited by
Desmond Hogan
Princeton University
Howard Williams
University of Cardiff
Allen Wood
Indiana University

KANT AND GLOBAL DISTRIBUTIVE JUSTICE

Sylvie Loriaux
Laval University, Canada

CAMBRIDGE
UNIVERSITY PRESS

CAMBRIDGE
UNIVERSITY PRESS

University Printing House, Cambridge CB2 8BS, United Kingdom

One Liberty Plaza, 20th Floor, New York, NY 10006, USA

477 Williamstown Road, Port Melbourne, VIC 3207, Australia

314–321, 3rd Floor, Plot 3, Splendor Forum, Jasola District Centre, New Delhi – 110025, India

79 Anson Road, #06–04/06, Singapore 079906

Cambridge University Press is part of the University of Cambridge.

It furthers the University's mission by disseminating knowledge in the pursuit of education, learning, and research at the highest international levels of excellence.

www.cambridge.org
Information on this title: www.cambridge.org/9781108729062
DOI: 10.1017/9781108678834

First published 2020

A catalogue record for this publication is available from the British Library.

ISBN 978-1-108-72906-2 Paperback
ISSN 2397-9461 (online)
ISSN 2514-3824 (print)

Cambridge University Press has no responsibility for the persistence or accuracy of URLs for external or third-party internet websites referred to in this publication and does not guarantee that any content on such websites is, or will remain, accurate or appropriate.

Kant and Global Distributive Justice

Elements in the Philosophy of Immanuel Kant

DOI: 10.1017/9781108678834
First published online: November 2020

Sylvie Loriaux
Laval University, Canada

Author for correspondence: Sylvie Loriaux, sylvie.loriaux@pol.ulaval.ca

Abstract: This Element argues that although Kant's political thought does not tackle issues of global poverty and inequality head on, it nonetheless offers important conceptual and normative resources to think of our global socioeconomic duties. It delves into the Kantian duty to enter a rightful condition beyond the state and shows that a proper understanding of this duty not only leads us to acknowledge a duty of right to assist states that are unable to fulfil the core functions of a state, but also provides valuable hints at what just transnational trade relations and a just regulation of immigration should look like.

Keywords: Immanuel Kant, beneficence, equality of opportunity, rightful condition, global poverty and inequality

ISBNs: 9781108729062 (PB), 9781108678834 (OC)
ISSNs: 2397-9461 (online), 2514-3824 (print)

Contents

1 Introduction

To talk about global distributive justice today is, above all, to talk about two main questions. The first question relates to the *nature* of our distributive duties on a global scale. Can our distributive duties toward the global poor properly be described as duties of beneficence, or should they also be considered duties of justice? This question is not merely conceptual, but is also likely to have significant normative implications. Duties of justice are indeed broadly assumed to be more stringent than duties of beneficence – they are in particular regarded as enjoying a priority and an enforceability that duties of beneficence lack. The second question relates to the *extent* of our distributive duties on a global scale. Even if we admit that global poverty is not simply a matter of beneficence, but also of justice, this does not yet solve the question as to how far our duties of justice extend on a global scale. Would socioeconomic justice be realized in the world if all inhabitants of the planet had enough to lead a minimally decent life (i.e., if absolute poverty were eradicated) or does it also require a reduction of those socioeconomic inequalities that persist above this level of sufficiency (i.e., a reduction of relative poverty)? It is worth noting in this regard that duties of distributive justice are today typically identified with duties of egalitarian justice, on the understanding that they do not necessarily require that resources be distributed in an equal way, but rather that inequalities of resources be justified.

These questions are obviously absent from Kant's political thought. At the domestic level, the issue of socioeconomic inequality is addressed only to specify that the principle of '*equality* with every other as a *subject*' requires the implementation of a certain form of equality of opportunity, but is also compatible with the greatest inequality in wealth (TP 8: 291–4).[1] As for the issue of absolute poverty relief, it features in only one passage of the *Doctrine of right*, which grants the state the right to levy taxes in order to help its members satisfy their most necessary needs (MM 6: 326), but which also seems to contradict the view that Kant supports elsewhere, namely that right, unlike beneficence, has nothing to do with human need (MM 6: 230). At the international level, no mention is made of (re)distribution of resources, which is not surprising when we consider that the contemporary reflection on global distributive justice has for a great part been triggered by the emergence of unprecedented international economic institutions.

---

[1] Citations of *Groundwork of The metaphysics of morals* (G), *On the common saying: That may be correct in theory, but it is of no use in practice* (TP), *Toward perpetual peace* (TPP), and *The metaphysics of morals* (MM) (which includes the *Doctrine of right* and the *Doctrine of virtue*) will be to the translations by Mary J. Gregor (1996).

Must we conclude that global distributive justice has no place in a Kantian political theory? There are reasons to think otherwise, and this is what this Element will strive to show. A first thing to note is indeed that, just like the vast majority of contemporary global justice thinkers, Kant insists on the idea that our global duties are not merely a matter of philanthropy or ethics, but are also a matter of right or justice. And just like them, he attributes to right a certain priority and a certain force. To begin with, he makes it clear that an action can hardly be called beneficent if it involves the violation of rights or if it is performed against a background of deep socioeconomic injustices. He also emphasizes that, unlike duties of virtue (among which the duty of beneficence), duties of right are duties for which external lawgiving and coercion are possible. A second thing to note is that the duty of right Kant insists upon in the global sphere is the duty to enter a rightful condition – a condition which he also describes as a 'condition of distributive justice' (MM 6: 307). To be sure, the expression 'distributive justice' does not, for Kant, connote egalitarian socioeconomic concerns (as it does today), but refers to the presence of public laws securing what belongs to each. Nevertheless, by affirming the existence of a duty of right to submit to public laws in the global sphere, Kant also affirms the existence of a duty of right to reform these laws so as to accord them with the idea of the original contract, that is, to ensure that these laws could possibly be consented to by all those global actors that are subject to them.

This Element will insist on the socioeconomic potential of this double-faceted duty of right. Its main objective will be to show that even if Kant's political thought does not tackle issues of global poverty and inequality head on, it nonetheless offers important conceptual and normative resources to think of our global socioeconomic duties. More precisely, it will argue that Kant's political thought offers, first, the resources to acknowledge, besides a duty of beneficence to help people in need, a duty of right to assist states that are unable to fulfil the core functions of a state, and second, valuable hints at what just transnational trade relations and a just regulation of immigration should look like.

The argument will proceed in three steps. The first section will address the question of global poverty on the basis of Kant's conception of the duty of beneficence. It will start by explicating the way in which Kant defines this duty as a duty of practical love and grounds it, on the one hand, in the impossibility of universalizing the maxim of indifference without contradiction, and on the other hand, in the absolute value of humanity as an end in itself. It will then delve into the forces and weaknesses of an approach to global poverty which takes Kant's conception of the duty of beneficence as its point of departure. It will show that helping people in need, far from being optional, is for Kant a universal moral duty, which rests on the recognition of the greatness of each human being and which has the potential to counter paternalistic abuses. As far as weaknesses are concerned, particular attention will be paid to the fact that Kant conceives of the duty of beneficence as a duty that is wide, non-enforceable, generative of status inequality, and especially, one whose fulfilment presupposes a baseline of justice. Concerning the latter point, Kant indeed makes the important claim that the inequalities of wealth that make beneficence both possible and necessary are 'for the most part' the result of the injustice of the government (MM 6: 454).

It is essentially to the elucidation of this claim that the second section will be devoted. Its aim will be to determine in which sense the introduction of wealth inequalities by the government can be considered unjust. The Kantian idea of the original contract will be of great importance in this undertaking. It is indeed by examining what kind of public laws could not possibly be consented to by free, equal, and independent citizens that two principles of domestic socioeconomic justice will emerge. The first is a principle of formal equality of opportunity, which demands that no subject be prevented by formal obstacles from rising in the social hierarchy because of their social origin. The second principle is a redistributive principle, which requires rich members of society to contribute, through redistributive taxes, to maintaining the existence of those members of society who are unable to maintain themselves. The last subsection of the second section will make the transition from domestic to global distributive justice by raising the question of the circumstances of distributive justice. It will invoke Kant's 'postulate of public right' to show that the Kantian circumstances of distributive justice obtain in the global sphere and enjoin us, first, to establish interstate and cosmopolitan public laws, and second, to continuously reform these laws so as to accord them with the idea of the original contract. The key question will then be to determine whether or not this accord involves the recognition of duties of right to combat certain forms of poverty and inequality in the global sphere.

This question will be at the heart of the third and last section. This section will start by clarifying the subject-matter of both interstate and cosmopolitan public right and by examining the complex nature of the Kantian duty to enter a rightful condition, which comprises both a conservative and an ideal dimension. The notion of 'provisional right' will be mobilized to show that the absence of a global coercive power does not exempt global actors from the duty to respect existing public laws and to reform these laws so as to bring them into conformity with the idea of the original contract or with rational right. Fulfilling this double-faceted duty is, on the contrary, the only way for them to demonstrate their willingness to enter a rightful condition beyond the state. The second part of the third section will examine the socioeconomic implications that the postulate of public right may have on a global scale by addressing the following two questions: 'Can rich states be said to have a duty of right to relieve global poverty?' and 'Can a global principle of formal equality of opportunity be invoked to condemn certain forms of global inequalities?' It will argue that Kantian states can be regarded as having a duty of right to assist those states that are unable to fulfil the core functions of a state. It will also argue that Kant's theory of cosmopolitan right offers valuable hints at what just transnational trade relations and a just regulation of immigration should look like. More specifically, it will show that it enjoins us, first, to fill the legal loopholes left by domestic and interstate public right; second, to devise global trade rules in such a way that they do not contradict the rights of all global actors involved (such as states' capacity to determine themselves); and third, to devise immigration laws in such a way that no inhabitant of the earth is denied access to inhabitable land. The conclusion will bring us back to the limitations of a beneficence-based approach to global poverty and inequality, and will examine to what extent a justice-based approach is able to overcome them.

2 A Duty of Beneficence to Help People in Need

That Kant recognizes the existence of a moral duty to assist people in need is beyond any doubt. As he clearly states in *The metaphysics of morals* (1797), 'To be beneficent, that is, to promote according to one's means the happiness of others in need, without hoping for something in return, is everyone's duty' (MM 6: 453), or already twenty-two years earlier in the *Groundwork of The metaphysics of morals* (1785), 'To be beneficent where one can is a duty' (G 4: 398).

Kant conceives of the duty of assistance or the duty of beneficence as one of the three forms that the more encompassing duty of love to other human beings can take, the other two forms being the duty of gratitude and the duty of sympathy (MM 6: 452). The duty of love to other human beings is not limited to situations of distress, but calls each of us more broadly to promote the end that all other human beings naturally pursue, namely their happiness. The happiness or the well-being of others is thus described as an end that is at the same time a duty for everyone, that is, as an end that everyone ought to regard and to promote as their own end (MM 6: 388; MM 6: 393). As a duty to adopt an end that is also a duty for each, the duty of love, and with it the duty of beneficence, constitutes what Kant calls a 'duty of virtue' (MM 6: 383).

It is important to notice the active or practical character of the duty of love to other human beings. The fact that it implies the adoption of an end and hence an 'internal act of the mind' (MM 6: 239) does not mean that it is a purely internal duty. In other words, the duty of love does not simply demand that we wish the happiness of others, which basically costs us nothing. The love that we are discussing here cannot be reduced to a wish, but concerns more fundamentally the maxim of actions, that is, the '*subjective* principle of action, a principle which the subject himself makes his rule (how he wills to act)' (MM 6: 225). More particularly, the duty of love to other human beings must 'be thought as the maxim of *benevolence* (practical love), which results in beneficence' (MM 6: 449).[2] It consists in an active benevolence and, as such, constitutes an external duty, that is, a duty that obliges us to perform external actions or *to do* something in order to promote the well-being of others (MM 6: 450).

The love that is one's duty to demonstrate is not a matter of feelings either: it is not a question of experiencing satisfaction at the sight of the happiness of others, which Kant identifies with a '*pathological* love' (G 4: 399) or '*delight* in them' (MM 6: 449; MM 6: 450). To be sure, as indicated, Kant also recognizes the existence of a duty of sympathy (which he also calls 'duty of humanity') and he conceives of it as a duty to cultivate our compassionate natural feelings and to actively take part in the fate of others, by, for instance, seeking the places where the poor are to be found (MM 6: 457). However, he also specifies that this duty is only 'indirect'. It finds its raison d'être in the fact that compassionate natural feelings can sometimes help us do what the representation of duty does not succeed in making us do on its own. Put differently, we have no duty to experience this or that feeling *as such*, but we have the duty to cultivate certain feelings *as means* to facilitate the fulfilment of other duties, in this case our duty of 'active and rational benevolence' (MM 6: 456).

Let us now consider the way in which Kant grounds the duty of beneficence. We can distinguish between two justifications or derivations. The first, which tends to dominate *The metaphysics of morals*, but which is also found already in the *Groundwork*, lays the emphasis on the impossibility of universalizing the maxim of self-interest without contradiction (G 4: 423; MM 6: 393; MM 6: 451; MM 6: 453). Thus Kant tells us that each human being wishes to be helped and therefore to be loved by others when they find themselves in need, or put differently, each human being makes of their well-being an end for

---

[2] By identifying the duty of love with the duty of beneficence, Kant seems in this quote to refer to a broader conception of the duty of beneficence, which goes beyond the provision of assistance to people in need and literally consists in 'doing good' or promoting the well-being of others. By contrast, when he presents the three duties of love in a more detailed way, he explicitly associates the duty of beneficence to situations of need (MM 6: 452–3). The duties of gratitude and sympathy appear, for their part, as duties whose fulfilment encourages the promotion of the well-being of others and hence the fulfilment of the duty of beneficence in both the broad and narrow senses. To take the example of gratitude, Kant tells us that it is an "opportunity" for the recipients of assistance to "cultivate [their] love of human beings" (MM 6: 456), while its contrary (ingratitude) "stands love of human beings on its head, as it were, and degrades absence of love into an authorization to hate the one who loves" (MM 6: 459). The link between the duty of sympathy and the duty of love will be discussed a bit later in the text.

others. Yet, since a maxim cannot oblige unless it possesses the universality of a law, and hence, unless it also makes the well-being of others an end for everyone, each human being must also demonstrate a practical love of others and help them when they find themselves in need. The maxim of common interest is, as a consequence, a universal duty for human beings. By contrast, the maxim of self-interest is contrary to duty because its universalization would deprive us of the help we all need, which would make the maxim conflict with itself (MM 6: 453)

The *Groundwork* offers valuable clarifications as to the nature of this contradiction. Kant indeed argues that the maxim of indifference to the needs of others could admittedly be conceived as a universal law of nature – a world devoid of beneficence would not in any way prevent the human race from surviving – but it could not be willed as a universal law of nature. As he puts it, 'a will that decided this would conflict with itself, since many cases could occur in which one would need the love and sympathy of others and in which, by such a law of nature arisen from his own will, he would rob himself of all hope of the assistance he wishes for himself' (G 4: 423). The contradiction to be elucidated is thus a 'contradiction in the will', and in view of this passage, it may be tempting to interpret it in a prudential way. It may indeed seem that the reason we have a duty to adopt the maxim of beneficence is that a refusal to do so would ultimately run against our own interests. The maxim of indifference to the needs of others would be a bad strategy to satisfy our own needs. However, this kind of interpretation is excluded from a Kantian framework: the moral acceptability of a maxim would otherwise vary from one person to another, according to what they would accept for themselves given the particular situation in which they find themselves. Prudence could, for instance, lead a person who is extremely rich, who has little aversion for risk, and who is surrounded by extremely poor persons to will that the maxim of indifference to the needs of others becomes a universal law.[3]

This point acquires a particular resonance in the context of global poverty and inequality. The condition that is required for a prudential foundation of a global 'duty' of assistance is indeed that a global practice of assistance can be considered truly advantageous by all parties concerned. However, given the scale of existing global inequalities, it is doubtful that the global poorest will, in the foreseeable future, be in a position to assist the global richest, and therefore, that the latter will have more to gain by adopting the maxim of beneficence than

---

[3] This is why the Silver Rule, 'Do *not* do unto others as you would *not* have them do unto you', cannot be regarded as providing a criterion for the moral acceptability of maxims. As Kant himself points out, many persons would indeed accept that others have no duty of beneficence toward them if they are also exempted from it (G 4: 430).

by adopting the maxim of indifference to the needs of others. As Brian Barry nicely illustrates, 'even if the USA were hit in one year by a major earthquake, a serious drought, and several disastrous hurricanes, it could still pull through economically by borrowing or realizing foreign assets. The probability, in the lifetime of anyone now alive, that the USA will be asking Bangladesh for aid is so low as to mean that aid from the USA simply cannot be constructed as mutual aid' (Barry 1989: 483). Under current circumstances, it would be imprudent for the global richest to adopt the maxim of beneficence since doing so would place them in the position of agents continuously providing assistance without ever receiving any assistance in return.

Another, more plausible interpretation of the contradiction in the will is in terms of what a human being could not possibly will *as a rational finite being.* As a *rational* being, every human being necessarily wills to attain certain ends. And since the idea of willing to attain an end comprises, in an analytical way, the idea of willing the means necessary to attain it, every human being also necessarily wills the means to attain their ends. But as a *finite* being, no human being can ever be sure that they will have the means to achieve their ends. They can, for instance, never have total control over their talents, their character traits, the resources available to them, and more generally, the way things are going. All these contingencies converge toward what Barbara Herman has called 'the ubiquity (inescapability) of the possibility of needing help' (Herman 1984: 584). The contradiction in the will here refers to the idea that a human being cannot will the maxim of indifference to hold as a universal law because, *as a rational finite being* who necessarily sets themselves ends they can never be sure to attain on their own, they cannot coherently will being systematically refused the help they need in order to attain their ends. According to Barbara Herman and Onora O'Neill, this interpretation takes us in fact to the limits or the preconditions of a human will, that is, to what a rational finite being must necessarily will if they are to will anything at all. To them, certain ends show up as 'necessary ends', that is, as ends that cannot be abandoned but must be realized if human beings are to remain rational, end-setting beings. Yet, as they go on to point out, human beings are also finite beings and can, as such, always end up in situations in which they need the help of others to realize the ends they cannot possibly forgo as rational beings. O'Neill talks in this regard of 'the survival of [our] agency' and more specifically, of 'an awareness of the limitations of [our] own agency, on which, all [our] plans for action (including the futile – or perhaps self-deceiving – plan of self-sufficiency) are premised' (O'Neill 1989: 348). She underlines the vulnerability of human beings and the fact that this vulnerability can result in their capacities to act being undercut and even destroyed (O'Neill 1989: 354). In the same vein, Herman frames her argument around the notion of 'true needs', which she understands as those needs that cannot be left unsatisfied if a human being is to function or continue to function as a rational agent (Herman 1984: 586, 597). Underlying both accounts is the idea that a human being cannot will the maxim of indifference to hold as a universal law because they cannot coherently will being deprived of the help that may prove necessary to achieve their necessary ends.

The *Groundwork* also presents a second way of grounding or deriving the existence of the duty of beneficence, namely, from the requirement to 'harmonize' or to positively agree with humanity as an 'end in itself' (G 4: 430). 'Humanity', in this context, no longer refers to the human race or to the properties of human beings as members of a biological species, but to 'rational nature', that is, to the capacity to act according to rational principles (whether moral or not) (G 4: 412; G 4: 428–9) or the 'capacity to set oneself an end – any end whatsoever' (MM 6: 392). Kant places on humanity thus understood an absolute or unconditional value. He points out that, unlike the ends that we set ourselves as effects of our actions and that have value only insofar as we give them value (i.e., a relative value), the existence of humanity possesses in itself an absolute value, which limits the freedom of action of all human beings (G 4: 428; G 4: 430–1; G 4: 438). As he puts it, 'the human being and in general every rational being *exists* as an end in itself, *not merely as a means* to be used by this or that will at its discretion' (G 4: 428). Following Christine Korsgaard, we may relate the absolute value of humanity or rational nature to its 'value-conferring status': the ends I set myself as effects of my actions have value only insofar as I give them value, and I have reason to give them value only to the extent that I also value (at least implicitly) my rational nature as the instance that sets and confers value to them (Korsgaard 1996: 123). And since this is the way in which each rational being necessarily views their existence – namely, as the source of all value or as an end in itself – it is also an objective principle of action, which holds for all rational beings (G 4: 429).

When he applies these considerations to the question of beneficence, Kant tells us that even if humanity could very well subsist in a world in which everyone only refrained from encroaching on what belongs to another, this would only be 'a negative and not a positive agreement with *humanity as an end in itself* unless everyone also tries, as far as he can, to further the ends of others. For, the ends of a subject who is an end in itself must as far as possible be also *my ends*, if that representation is to have its *full* effect in me' (G 4: 430). A complete recognition of humanity or rational nature implies that we both negatively and positively respect it as an end in itself. On the one hand, we have the duty not to compromise its existence or the possibility of its exercise by using it as a mere means. This mainly excludes the use of deception and coercion in our relations to others (Wood 2008: 87). On the other hand, we also have the duty to positively promote the happiness of others. It is indeed only by making the ends of others also our ends – that is, by helping them to pursue their own ends – that we come to fully appreciate the value of their rational nature as a self-existent and objectively valuable end. The underlying idea is that we cannot remain indifferent to the furtherance of the ends of others without also treating these ends as unworthy of consideration, and therefore, without lacking respect for the standing of others as ultimate sources of value.

2.1 Strengths of the Kantian Conception of the Duty of Beneficence

For those concerned about global poverty and inequality, the Kantian conception of the duty of beneficence offers important conceptual and normative resources. The first, which may seem obvious, but remains nonetheless important, is that it goes beyond the realm of supererogation. While assistance is often equated with simple generosity or a kind of moral extra which anyone is free to practice or not, Kant affirms its morally obligatory character. Those who adopt the maxim of beneficence are not going 'beyond duty'. They are not doing something that is good, but that it would actually not be bad not to do. Those who adopt the maxim of beneficence fulfil their moral duty, and it would be morally blameworthy for them not to do so. Admittedly – and we will come back to this later – Kant recognizes that it is morally permissible to choose how to fulfil one's duty of beneficence, and hence what specific actions of beneficence to perform. The duty of beneficence is said to be wide in that it does not indicate with any precision in what way and to what extent it ought to be fulfilled. Still, it is not morally permissible 'to make exceptions to the maxim of actions' (MM 6: 390) – that is, to impose on others the adoption of the maxim of beneficence, while allowing oneself to act on the maxim of indifference to the needs of others – since, as we have seen, a maxim cannot oblige unless it possesses the universality of a law. The transgression of wide duties becomes a vice when we 'make it [our] principle not to comply with such duties' (ibid.), as when, for example, we erect the principle of non-beneficence into our principle of action and refuse to make the happiness of others our own end.

In his groundbreaking article 'Famine, Affluence, and Morality', Peter Singer clearly highlights the urgency to revise our conceptual scheme and to regard assistance to those in extreme need as a matter of moral duty rather than as a matter of supererogation (Singer 1972: 235–6). It must be admitted that Singer's conception of the duty of assistance is on several points irreconcilable with Kant's – most notably because it makes it a duty to perform specific actions of beneficence (such as giving money to charities), and not only to act on the maxim of beneficence, not to mention his utilitarian claim that 'we ought to give until we reach the level of marginal utility – that is, the level at which, by giving more, I would cause as much suffering to myself or my dependents as I would relieve by my gift' (Singer 1972: 241). But the point on which Singer agrees with Kant is that helping people in extreme need is neither optional nor merely good, but is everyone's moral duty.

This leads us to a second aspect of the Kantian conception of the duty of beneficence which deserves to be emphasized, namely its universality: 'the maxim of benevolence (practical love of human beings) is a duty of all human beings toward one another, whether or not one finds them worthy of love' (MM 6: 450). Since the duty of beneficence is ultimately grounded in certain characteristics inherent to the very human condition, its scope can have no principled geographical, political, or cultural limitations. The practical love of human beings is a universal duty because human beings are all identical in respect of the features that prevent the maxim of non-beneficence from being universalized: they are all equally 'rational beings with needs, united by nature in one dwelling place so that they can help one another' (MM 6: 453). Certainly, it may be easier to respond to the needs of those who are geographically or emotionally closer. We may be in a better position to identify their true needs and to respond to them effectively. But what justifies our duty to help them in the first place is not our geographical or emotional proximity, but rather the impossibility for rational finite beings to will the maxim of non-beneficence to hold as a universal law, or to put in terms of the second derivation, what justifies the duty of beneficence is the recognition of the absolute value of humanity, and hence of every single human being.

A third strength of the Kantian conception of the duty of beneficence, which is brought into relief by the second derivation, is the emphasis it places on the greatness rather than the finitude of the poor. Admittedly, this claim calls for some nuance. It is true that there would be no occasion activating a duty of assistance if human beings were all invulnerable beings or beings without needs. It is also true that Kant's first derivation of the duty of beneficence explicitly refers to the idea that 'everyone who finds himself in need wishes to be helped by others' (MM 6: 453) and that 'many cases could occur in which one would need the love and sympathy of others' (G 4: 423). However, the second derivation suggests that the duty of assistance is ultimately grounded not in the recognition of human finitude as such, but rather in the recognition of human dignity, that is, in the recognition that a human being is a rational being and possesses as such an unconditional value that must be respected and affirmed by everyone. Instead of being presented as passive victims, who are lacking certain things and who need others to provide these to them, the poor are illuminated in their greatness as instantiations of a rational nature whose absolute value must always be honoured.

As Nancy Fraser has recently shown, the way in which the recipients of aid are presented is not without consequences (Fraser 2010: 369). According to her, by depicting them as passive victims, who simply lack the means of subsistence, we tend to disregard their status as agents and as potential political actors. We also tend to conceal the broader network of interactions in which they are embedded and the various ways in which this network may be connected to their poverty. Or to put it another way, by presenting the poor as passive victims, we may neglect their agency, but also the agency of potential providers of aid, and more particularly, the fact that potential providers of aid may be actively involved in the very existence of the poverty they have the duty of beneficence to alleviate. As we will see later, this intuition is shared by Kant since he explicitly acknowledges that the very fact of being in need of help or of being in a position to help may be the result of background injustices.

A final and far from least important aspect of the Kantian conception of the duty of beneficence is its potential to counter paternalistic abuses. Critical voices are regularly raised against international aid initiatives that pay insufficient attention to the way in which local populations themselves conceive of their needs and to the knowledge they have accumulated through generations (Dübgen 2012). More particularly, some people question the moral acceptability of the practice of aid conditionality – a practice that makes the grant of international aid conditional on requirements of 'good governance', which can be intrusive, especially when political and economic reforms are involved (Collingwood 2003). Even if the imposition of certain conditions may seem necessary to ensure that the aid provided will indeed reach those who really need it, it must be recognized that it can also be an open door to external interference and undermine the right of recipient states to decide for themselves what purposes they want to achieve and how they want to achieve them.

Kant is well aware that alleged actions of beneficence can be accompanied by or translate into a denial of right and freedom. This is what emerges from his claim that the human race could probably better subsist without beneficence 'than when everyone prates about sympathy and benevolence and even exerts himself to practice them occasionally, but on the other hand also cheats where he can, sells the right of human beings or otherwise infringes upon it' (G 4: 423). His answer consists in establishing a normative priority between duties of love and duties of right. As he specifies in *Toward perpetual peace*, although love of human beings and respect for their rights are both duties, only the latter is an unconditional duty or a duty that commands absolutely. The duty of love, by contrast, must be considered conditional to the duty to respect rights in the sense that those who want to promote the well-being of another must make sure that they do not violate that person's rights (TPP 8: 385–6). This normative priority is in fact already contained in Kant's very definition of the duty of beneficence. To say that beneficence consists in making the ends of others my own ends is indeed to say that 'I cannot do good to anyone in accordance with *my* concepts of happiness' (MM 6: 454). It is impossible for me to be beneficent toward a person if I fail to respect the way they themselves conceive of their well-being or happiness; otherwise, I would not only fail to promote their ends and hence to be truly beneficent, but I would also behave in a unjust way because I would infringe on their external freedom – a freedom that Kant basically understands as a freedom to 'seek his happiness in the way that seems good to him, provided he does not infringe upon that freedom of others to strive for a like end which can coexist with the freedom of everyone in accordance with a possible universal law' (TP 8: 290).

It is worth mentioning that some other thinkers share Kant's idea that the duty of beneficence is fundamentally concerned with the promotion of the well-being of others and is thus goal-based, but draw from it a different conclusion, more prone to paternalism: namely, that recipients of aid are expected to use the resources they receive in a way deemed appropriate by benefactors. This is, for instance, the view espoused by Brian Barry, who stresses that insofar as benefactors are the true owners of their resources, they are entitled to determine for what purposes these resources are to be used and whether the use made of them does effectively serve these purposes (Barry 1982: 247–8). If they consider that their funds are not spent in an appropriate way, they are perfectly free to cut them. Barry could be interpreted as focusing on a limitation that Kant mentions only in passing: it is for others to decide what their happiness consists of, 'but it is open to me to refuse them many things that *they* think will make them happy but that I do not, as long as they have no right to demand them from me as what is theirs' (MM 6: 388). By granting benefactors the right to refuse another what they do not regard as belonging to that other person's happiness, this passage may suggest that it is ultimately up to benefactors to decide how the happiness of others is to be understood. However, to say that I may refuse to give certain things to another is not to say that I may impose on them my own conception of happiness. Kant's concern in making the above claim seems to be that we cannot have a duty to perform an action that we sincerely believe to be unconducive to another's happiness. But the key idea he otherwise puts forward, and which Barry tends to pass over in silence, is that from the moment we want to practice beneficence or to make the well-being of another our end, we cannot gloss over the way in which potential recipients themselves conceive of this end. The reason for this is not simply that taking our recipient's views into account is likely to make our aid more effective, but also and more fundamentally, that there can be no respect for freedom and hence no beneficence without taking recipients' views into account.

If one were to sum up the main conceptual and normative resources that the Kantian conception of the duty of beneficence provides us for addressing the issue of global poverty and inequality, one could say that it presents the provision of aid to the needy as a moral duty whose scope has no principled geographical frontiers and which brings into relief the greatness of each human being, while respecting their right to freedom.

2.2 Limitations of the Kantian Conception of the Duty of Beneficence

However, the Kantian conception of the duty of beneficence also involves important limitations. So, the fact that the duty of beneficence is characterized as a universal duty does of course not mean that everyone has a duty to help all others in the same way. To begin with, the practical character of the duty of beneficence makes this impossible. Given that beneficence, unlike mere benevolence, requires *doing* something, it cannot possibly be without limits. We can certainly wish the happiness of *all* others, but by our external actions, we can only advance the happiness of *some* others. We cannot but miss some occasions to help or do good to others. Kant also admits that once external actions, and not merely wishes, are at stake, the degree of beneficence may vary according to the diversity of the persons who are loved: 'I can, without violating the universality of the maxim, vary the degree greatly in accordance with the different objects of my love (one of whom concerns me more closely than another)' (MM 6: 452). Put differently, even though I cannot 'make exceptions to the maxim of actions' – in this case, the general and indeterminate maxim of beneficence – I can 'limit one maxim of duty by another', that is, I can limit one specific way of practicing beneficence (e.g., love of human beings in general) by another (e.g., love of one's parents) (MM 6: 390; Hill 2002: 221). More fundamentally, and as already indicated, the 'wideness' of the duty of beneficence means that everyone retains a certain latitude as to the precise way to fulfil it (MM 6: 388–90). This wideness stems from the fact that the duty of beneficence is above all a duty to act upon a maxim: 'if the law can prescribe only the maxim of actions, not actions themselves, this is a sign that it leaves a playroom (*latitudo*) for free choice in following (complying with) the law, that is, that the law cannot specify precisely in what way one is to act and how much one is to do by the action for an end that is also a duty' (MM 6: 390). The moral law demands that we subordinate the ends we have to the ends we ought to have, but it leaves us free to decide how precisely to do so (MM 6: 389).

The difficulty that the wideness of the duty of beneficence poses for the issue of global poverty is that it seems to entail that the global rich could adequately fulfil their duty of beneficence without ever performing any concrete action in order to improve the lot of the global poor, provided they do not make it their principle to act in an egoistic way, but regularly provide assistance to others, whether rich or poor, close or distant. This difficulty is reinforced by what can be called the expressive nature of the duty of beneficence. As we have seen, this duty can be regarded as a duty to positively respect humanity as an end in itself. Unlike all other ends, humanity is not an end 'to be produced' or a mere subjective end whose existence has value *for us*, but it is a self-standing (*selbstständig*) end, that is, an end whose existence has in itself an *absolute value* and ought to be respected wherever it is found (G 4: 437) (Wood 2008: 85). Yet, as far as respect is concerned, there are no half measures: either an action respects humanity or it does not, and among the many actions that promote the well-being of others and hence the many ways of positively respecting humanity in others, none seems to deserve priority on the ground that it would be 'more respectful' of humanity than another. More particularly, the Kantian conception of the duty of beneficence does not seem able to account for situations of urgency that leave little, or even no, latitude for free choice. If I encounter a person whose life is in danger and if I am the only one who could save their life without having to suffer any significant costs, I can hardly excuse my inaction by claiming that I will help other persons on other occasions or that I do not make it my principle of action to be indifferent to the needs of others.

One may be tempted to try to overcome this difficulty by attributing a particular moral importance to the material preconditions of rational agency and by distinguishing between two ways of positively respecting humanity in others: on the one hand, by helping them to satisfy their basic or true needs (*beneficence in the narrow sense*); on the other hand, by promoting their ends beyond a minimal threshold of well-being, for instance by doing them a service or a favour (*beneficence in the broad sense*).[4] This way of proceeding could be in line with the first derivation of the duty of beneficence, namely the derivation that centres on the impossibility of universalizing the maxim of non-beneficence without contradiction, especially if the help of others is presented as necessary for the very survival of human agency. But the second derivation, which rests on the respect owed to humanity as an end in itself, by bringing into

---

[4] Such a distinction between a broad duty of beneficence to 'do good' to others and a more specific duty of humanity to alleviate suffering is made by Barry (1982) and Tom D. Campbell (1974).

relief the greatness of each human being, makes it at the same time difficult to justify any normative priority between different ways of being beneficent.

A second limitation of the Kantian conception of the duty of beneficence concerns the possibility of external constraint. Human nature being what it is, it goes without saying that a great deal of human basic needs would remain unsatisfied if their satisfaction were entirely left to the good will of potential benefactors. At the domestic level, the solution typically consists in implementing a system of taxation and in forcing those who are richer to redistribute part of their wealth to those who are poorer, be it directly in cash or indirectly through a public health care or education system. In the next section, we will see that Kant's *Doctrine of right* grants states the right to levy taxes in order to maintain those members of society who are unable to maintain themselves. But as far as the duty of beneficence is concerned, Kant denies that external constraint is morally possible (MM 6: 383). Even if he recognizes that the duty of beneficence obliges us to perform external actions and is therefore an 'external duty', he also emphasizes that its lawgiving can only be internal (MM 6: 220). Given that the duty of beneficence is a duty to adopt an end and that the adoption of an end can only be an 'internal act of the mind' – a constraint that one freely exercises on oneself (a 'free self-constraint') – it quite naturally escapes the possibility of an external constraint and thus also the reach of positive law (MM 6: 239; MM 6: 383).

It could be objected that even if a person cannot be compelled to make the well-being of others their own end, that person can be compelled to perform external actions that promote the well-being of others. As Allen Buchanan points out, one cannot force a person 'to *be* charitable' or 'to have a certain disposition of character', but one can very well force them to act in a charitable way (Buchanan 1987: 569). Likewise, Kant does not deny that '[a]nother can indeed *coerce* me *to do* something that is not my end (but only a means to another's end)' (MM 6: 381), nor that an external lawgiving 'may prescribe external actions that lead to an end without the subject making it his end' (MM 6: 239). But the problem that resurfaces when one tries to apply this reasoning to the duty of beneficence is that of paternalism. To impose by force a duty that, like the duty of beneficence, is a wide duty – and hence a duty that is indeterminate as to the amount and kind of assistance to be provided – can give rise to arbitrariness and abuses. Alexander Kaufman sums it up well: 'the right to act in accordance with a duty of beneficence could significantly expand the sovereign's coercive power without specifying a criterion to limit that power. Moreover, since the duty is broad, the right/obligation to comply with such duty could encourage sovereigns to engage in paternalistic meddling' (Kaufman 1999: 28). This problem would remain even if one were to prioritize true needs because, as Kant put is, what is truly a need for a person depends on their sensibilities and they must be left to decide this for themselves (MM 6: 393).

A third limitation relates to the status inequality that develops between those who provide assistance and those who receive assistance. Even if the Kantian duty of beneficence implies respect for the freedom of recipients and affirms the absolute value of their humanity, it does not exclude all forms of dependence or feelings of inferiority. As Kant acknowledges, the poor can very much depend on the will of the rich for their welfare (TP 8: 292), and this dependence can generate in them a feeling of humiliation and a loss of self-respect – a loss which can be further exacerbated by the 'meritorious' character that is often attributed, including by Kant, to the duty of beneficence. This meritorious character indeed means that by providing assistance, benefactors also put their recipients under obligation, imposing upon them a duty of gratitude (MM 6: 448; MM 6: 450; MM 6: 454–6). It is in order to counter the harmful effects that actions of beneficence can have on their recipients that Kant insists on the importance of uniting the duty of love and the duty of respect into one duty (MM 6: 448). Those who provide assistance must allow their recipients to keep the self-respect they may legitimately claim given the absolute value of their humanity (MM 6: 462). They must therefore limit their self-esteem by refraining from using others as mere means allowing them to revel in moral feelings (MM 6: 449–50; MM 6: 453). They must also refrain from considering their beneficence as a meritorious duty and present it instead as a mere debt (as something that is owed to others) or as a small friendly service, or even better, provide it in complete secrecy (MM 6: 448–9; MM 6: 453). Still, in spite of these recommendations, Kant concedes that inequalities between benefactors and recipients will never be completely eliminated. Recipients will never be able to repay the benefits they received because they will never be able to compensate the '*priority* of merit' enjoyed by benefactors, who were the first to practice beneficence. As Kant puts it, 'the obligation with regard to it cannot be discharged completely by any act in keeping with it (so that one who is under obligation always remains under obligation)' (MM 6: 455). If we apply these considerations to the issue of global poverty, the main lesson to be drawn is that beneficence brings with it an inequality of status which, even if it must and can be mitigated, will never be completely removed: the global poor will always remain under obligation toward their rich benefactors.

A last limitation is that the fulfilment of the duty of beneficence presupposes a baseline of justice: we cannot be beneficent toward a person by providing them with goods we are not entitled to in the first place. As Kant puts it,

> Having the resources to practice such beneficence as depends on the goods of fortune is, for the most part, a result of certain human beings being favored through the injustice of the government, which introduces an inequality of wealth that makes others need their beneficence. Under such circumstances, does a rich man's help to the needy, on which he so readily prides himself as something meritorious, really deserve to be called beneficence at all? (MM 6: 454)

Even if our action does, as a matter of fact, advance the well-being of another person, it cannot be considered an action of beneficence, and hence a meritorious action, if it is performed against a background of injustice. This can be clearly seen in the case of rectificatory justice. There can be no merit in giving to a poor person the money we previously stole from them since this would only amount to returning what already belongs to them. But we may also take a broader perspective and doubt that the provision of assistance by a rich person to a poor person can properly be regarded as an action of beneficence when the inequalities that make this action possible, or even necessary, are themselves the result of unjust social institutions. We may, in other words, shift the attention from rectificatory to distributive justice and question the justice of the initial distribution of property rights. As Barry puts it, 'To talk about what I ought, as a matter of humanity, to do with what is mine makes no sense until we have established what is mine in the first place' (Barry 1982: 249). And what Kant seems to be saying in the above passage is that the existing distribution of property rights depends 'for the most part' on the injustice of the government and is therefore largely unjust. This claim raises two important questions: (1) In what sense can the introduction of wealth inequalities by the government constitute an injustice? (2) Does the recognition of such an injustice imply the recognition of a duty of right (and not only of beneficence) to alleviate socioeconomic inequalities or at least absolute poverty?

These questions will be at the heart of the next section, which can be seen as a transitional section moving from the issue of global beneficence to that of global distributive justice. The primary aim of this section will be to reconstruct Kant's views on domestic distributive or socioeconomic justice and to circumscribe the main arguments he offers in favour of duties of right to combat certain forms of poverty and inequality. The underlying assumption is that if global distributive justice is to have any place in Kant's political theory, then these arguments must be expected to play a central role in it. It may indeed be possible for us to have distributive duties toward our compatriots that we do not have toward foreigners. But is it very unlikely that we could have distributive duties toward foreigners that we do not have toward our compatriots. While going through this reconstruction, it will be helpful to bear in mind the limitations of an approach to global poverty that is based on the Kantian conception of the duty of beneficence, namely, the fact that beneficence represents a wide and non-enforceable duty, which is generative of status inequality and whose fulfilment presupposes a baseline of justice. This will allow us to subsequently determine whether and to what extent an approach formulated in terms of distributive justice is able to overcome these limitations.

3 Poverty and Inequality as Issues of Domestic Justice

This section mainly aims to show that, besides a duty of beneficence, Kant also recognizes duties of right to combat certain forms of poverty and inequality. What duties of right have in common with duties of virtue (including the duty of beneficence) is that they all relate to moral laws or laws of freedom, that is, to laws that are *a priori* valid for human actions. But they differ with regard to the kind of freedom they are related to. While duties of virtue concern freedom in both the internal and the external uses of choice and involve moral laws for principles of action or maxims, duties of right concern freedom only in the external use of choice and involve moral laws only for external actions (MM 6: 214; MM 6: 388–9). More precisely, duties of right primarily consist in limiting the external freedom of each so that it can coexist with the external freedom of all others in accordance with universal laws (TP 8: 289–90; MM 6: 230–1). Another important and related distinction is that duties of right are closely connected to the authorization to use coercion (MM 6: 231–3). Unlike duties of virtue, which require the adoption of an end and hence a self-constraint, duties of right are duties that can be given by external laws and to the fulfilment of which one can be coerced (MM 6: 220; MM 6: 379; MM 6: 383; MM 6: 394). This connection with coercion is in fact contained in the very concept of right since right amounts to limiting external freedoms so that they can coexist in accordance with universal laws, and the limitation of external freedom by the choice of another consists in a coercion (TP 8: 289–90; MM 6: 231). External laws are thus none other than laws of coercion that are to limit uses of freedom that are hindrances to freedom in accordance with universal laws.

In the reconstruction of Kant's conception of distributive justice that follows, a central place is given to the idea of the 'original contract'. It is first shown that this idea provides the criterion for assessing the justice of domestic public laws, and correlatively, that domestic socioeconomic injustices are mainly to be understood in terms of domestic public laws that a whole people could not possibly consent to. It is then argued that the idea of the original contract allows us to identify two principles of domestic distributive or socioeconomic justice. The first, which is embedded in Kant's critique of hereditary nobility, is a principle of formal equality of opportunity. The second, which emerges from Kant's discussion of the right of the state to levy taxes, is a principle of wealth redistribution in favour of those members of society who are unable to maintain their existence. The final subsection of this section makes the transition from domestic to global distributive justice by raising the question of the circumstances of distributive justice.

3.1 The Idea of the Original Contract as the Criterion of Justice for Public Laws

When using the phrase 'original contract', Kant does not refer to an empirical act that would have occurred at a given point in history and through which human beings would actually have consented to establish a political society. On the contrary, he even specifies that 'it is by no means necessary that this contract... be presupposed as a *fact* (as a fact it is indeed not possible)' (TP 8: 297). When Kant appeals to the original contract, he rather refers to the idea of the act through which a people constitutes itself into a state, and correlatively, to *'the state in idea*, as it ought to be in accordance with pure principles of right', an idea that 'serves as a norm (*norma*) for every actual union into a commonwealth (hence serves as a norm for its internal constitution)' (MM 6: 313). The state in idea, which Kant identifies with the republican state, represents a kind of ideal state toward which every actual state is required to tend and whose constitution results from a certain kind of contract between its constituent members. One of its defining features is that its constitution treats its subjects as ends in themselves, that is, as citizens who participate in the legislative activity and who must, as a result, be able to consent to the external laws that govern their interactions (MM 6: 345).

As the idea of the act through which a people constitutes itself into a state and on which the external lawgiving of a people must be based, the idea of the original contract also constitutes 'the touchstone of any public law's conformity with right' (TP 8: 297), or to put it differently, the criterion of justice for positive law. It is this idea that allows us to assess whether or not a public law accords with natural right understood as rational right or right that each human being can conceive *a priori* through their reason (MM 6: 296). Put briefly, a public law cannot be considered just or conform to right if it is impossible for a whole people to consent to it (TP 8: 297). Conversely, a public law is to be considered just if it is possible for a whole people to consent to it. The latter may happen even if the whole people does not actually consent to the law in question, provided there is no contradiction for it to consent to it. Thus, even if the original contract is devoid of any empirical or historical meaning, it nevertheless possesses, as an idea of reason, a practical reality in that it obliges, on the one hand, each lawgiver to legislate in such a way that its laws could have emerged from the united will of the whole people, and on the other hand, each subject to regard themselves as having participated in the general agreement of this will (ibid.).

Let us stop for a moment at the notion of possible consent. Kant mentions several types of public laws to which, according to him, it would be impossible for a whole people to consent, namely, a law authorizing contracts of slavery (TP 8: 293; MM 6: 283; MM 6: 330), a law granting certain subjects the hereditary privilege of being noble (TP 8: 292–3; TP 8: 297; TPP 8: 350–1; MM 6: 328–9), a law distributing war contributions in an arbitrary unequal way (TP 8: 297), and a law prescribing that we consider a given ecclesiastical constitution as definitive, once it has been established (TP 8: 304–5). We can, however, wonder about the precise sense in which these quite different public laws could not possibly be consented to by a whole people, and as a result, be considered conform to right. It is indeed clear that the consent under consideration here cannot be interpreted in terms of actual consent, since it is not impossible for a whole people to actually consent to a law authorizing slavery contracts or prescribing that one regards a given ecclesiastical constitution as definitive. What then allows Kant to say that a whole people could not possibly consent to such laws?

To answer that question, it is necessary to examine more closely the nature of the contracting parties, in this case citizens as members of the state united to legislate. More particularly, attention must be paid to what Kant calls the 'attributes of a citizen, inseparable from his essence', namely, lawful freedom, civil equality, and civil independence (MM 6: 314). It must be noted that, as with the republican state, these attributes can fail to be recognized in real life, and that their recognition rather consists in an ideal toward which any actual external lawgiving must tend. They represent the principles according to which the republican constitution is instituted and hence the principles according to which any actual civil constitution ought to be instituted (TPP 8: 349–50). The 'attributes of a citizen' derive in fact from the 'innate and inalienable rights belonging necessarily to humanity' (TPP 8: 350) and can be considered as their 'civil expression' (Wood 2007: 194). They echo the way in which, in the *Introduction to the doctrine of right*, Kant explicates the innate right to freedom and shows that the rights to equality and to independence are not really distinct from it, but are already contained in it (MM 6: 237–8).[5] He tells us in this context that each human being possesses by nature – that is, independently of

---

[5] Note, however, that the attribute of civil independence is not mentioned in *Toward perpetual peace*, and that we find instead, next to freedom and equality, the '*dependence* of all upon a single common legislation' (TPP 8: 349–50).

any rightful deed (*rechtlich Akt*) – a right to '*[f]reedom* (independence from being constrained by another's choice), insofar as it can coexist with the freedom of every other in accordance with a universal law'. Each human being also possesses this right in an *equal* way in the sense that no one can be bound by others to more than they can in turn bind them. Lastly, the innate right to freedom also already includes the 'quality of being [one's] own master (*sui iuris*)', a quality that Kant elsewhere relates to the notion of independence (TP 8: 294–5).

What a consideration of the attributes inseparable from the essence of a citizen reveals to us is that in order to decide whether or not a public law is in accordance with right, we must not ask whether a whole people could actually consent to it – not even whether it would consent to it if placed in a hypothetical situation deemed relevant – but whether it may consent to it, that is, whether it is morally authorized to do so given its duty to respect the innate rights possessed by each human being.[6] Note in this regard that duties of right are not limited to duties to others, but also comprise a duty to oneself in one's relations to others – a duty which derives from the 'right of humanity in our own person' and which demands not to make oneself into a mere means for others, but always also to be an end for them (MM 6: 236). Importantly, this duty of 'rightful honor' shows that there are moral limits to what a human being may voluntarily consent to. To take the example of a public law authorizing slavery contracts, the reason why a whole people could not possibly consent to it is that its constituent members are human beings and that a human being is not morally authorized to renounce being a person and to make themselves into the property of another through a contract. A person must, on the contrary, always affirm the absolute value of their humanity in their relations to others. By depriving one of their personality, such a contract would deprive them of all their rights, including the right to conclude a contract, and would thus destroy itself (TP 8: 292; MM 6: 283; MM 6: 330).

3.2 Kant's Critique of Hereditary Nobility

Of particular interest to the question of socioeconomic injustice is the attribute of civil equality. Although it appears under different denominations in *The metaphysics of morals*, *Toward perpetual peace*, and *On the common saying*,

---

[6] Onora O'Neill has clearly shown how the consent under consideration differs both from an actual consent and from a hypothetical consent, and must be understood as a 'doubly modal' consent: justice *requires* the rejection of public laws that *cannot* possibly be consented to (O'Neill 2015: 181–2). At the heart of her interpretation, we find the idea that a constitution that fails to protect the freedom of individuals could not be universally consented to because by undermining freedom, it would also undermine the very possibility of consent (ibid. 178).

its content remains basically the same.[7] It essentially refers to the equal subjection to external laws of all members of the state and, correlatively, to their equal right to coerce one another (through public law). Human beings are equal as subjects in the sense that none of them can coerce others to more than what they can in turn be coerced (TP 8: 292). Importantly, it is when he discusses the attribute of civil equality that Kant comes to explicitly criticize certain forms of socioeconomic inequalities. His main target is undoubtedly 'hereditary nobility', which grants certain individuals, merely by virtue of their birth, various legal advantages or special rights, for instance an exclusive access to certain privileged positions in the bureaucracy, economy, or army. Hereditary nobility thus establishes a hierarchy between subjects, where some are born to command and others are born to obey. Kant firmly denies that it is in conformity with right to recognize such a hereditary nobility. He recalls that each human being possesses the same innate right to freedom and argues that since birth is not a deed, and *a fortiori* not a rightful deed, it cannot generate any 'inequality of rightful condition', that is, it cannot provide any reason to grant different rights to different persons or to subject different persons to different coercive laws (TP 8: 293). If certain subjects were authorized to transmit to their descendants the privilege of their condition and to thus eternally prevent others from reaching higher levels of the hierarchy, they would be authorized to coerce others *by their irresistible will*, as if birth had conferred certain legal advantages upon them. They would be authorized to coerce others 'without others in turn being able to coerce [them] by their reaction, and would rise above the level of a fellow subject' (TP 8: 293). To put it in terms of the original contract, a whole people could not possibly consent to a public law granting certain subjects the hereditary privilege of being noble because 'we cannot admit that any human being would throw away his freedom' (MM 6: 329).

Kant also formulates his argument in terms of merit. He argues that the general will of a people could not possibly agree that the rank granted by the state precedes merit because this would provide 'no basis to hope for merit' (TPP 8: 351; MM 6: 329). Nature is indeed such that talent and will, far from being hereditary, must generally be acquired by subjects themselves. Still, when we take a closer look, it seems that the idea that ultimately underpins this argument is not simply that a person's legal advantages should reflect their talent and will, but above all that they should not depend on the irresistible will of others or that no subject should 'coercively prevent others from attaining'

---

[7] Thus, *Toward perpetual peace* refers both to the equality of the members of a society '*as citizens of a state*' and to 'the right of equality of all citizens of a state as subjects' (TPP 8: 351), whereas *On the common saying* talks of the '*equality* [of each member of a state] as a subject' (TP 8: 290) and *The metaphysics of morals* of 'civil *equality*' (MM 6: 314).

them, as if they were qualified by birth for these advantages (TP 8: 293). This indeed follows from the place Kant gives to considerations of luck. As he explains in the following passage: 'He can be considered happy in that condition provided he is aware that, if he does not reach the same level as others, the fault lies only in himself ([his lack of] ability or earnest will) or circumstances for which he cannot blame any other, but not in the irresistible will of others who, as his fellow subjects in this condition, have no advantage over him as far as right is concerned' (TP 8: 293–4). What matters is that a subject's legal disadvantages do not depend on factors for which another subject can be held responsible. On this point, Kant departs from contemporary 'luck egalitarians' who deem it unjust for a person to be socially advantaged or disadvantaged because of good or bad luck – that is, because of factors for which one cannot be held responsible – and who demand that the effects of such factors on a person's life prospects be as much as possible neutralized.[8] Unlike these authors, Kant insists less on a person's own responsibility for their social position than on others' responsibility. What should be neutralized or eliminated are rank inequalities that are said to be innate and that therefore depend on the irresistible will of another. At this point, one may of course wonder about the distinction that Kant draws between considerations of luck and considerations of birth. How can he at the same time claim that a person's access to a higher social position may legitimately be determined by luck and deny that it can be conferred by birth? If the reason why birth cannot provide any legal advantages is that it is not a deed, it is difficult to see why the same would not also hold for luck. The most plausible way of overcoming this apparent difficulty is to distinguish between two facets of birth – social origin and natural talents – and to interpret Kant in light of traditional meritocracy.[9] On this reading, subjects could legitimately be rewarded for their qualifications, which are always in part the result of their natural talents and hence of luck, but they could not legitimately be excluded from a higher social position because of factors that have nothing to do with their qualifications, such as their social origin.

3.3 Formal Equality of Opportunity as a Principle of Distributive Justice

Kant's critique of hereditary nobility suggests that he endorses a principle of 'formal equality of opportunity'. This principle, which can also be expressed by the formula 'careers open to talent', concerns the rules that govern access to

---

[8] For defences of luck egalitarianism, see for instance: Richard Arneson (1989), G. A. Cohen (1989), Ronald Dworkin (2002), and John E. Roemer (1998).

[9] On the difference between contemporary luck egalitarianism and traditional meritocracy, see: Andrew Mason (2001).

advantaged social positions and basically requires, first, that all candidates be judged according to the same criteria and, second, that these criteria reflect considerations that are relevant given the nature of the positions under consideration. No formal barriers such as legal restrictions can prevent a qualified person from competing and occupying a given advantaged social position. This position must be accessible to all those who possess the required qualifications instead of being reserved only for those who are born from such or such parents. Insofar as it pronounces itself on the just allocation of advantaged social positions and so places limits on the kind of socioeconomic inequalities that can be justified, the principle of formal equality of opportunity can be regarded as a principle of egalitarian distributive justice (in the contemporary sense of the term).[10] Accordingly, Kant appears to be not only an 'egalitarian about *human worth'* (Wood 2007: 194), but also an egalitarian about the distribution of certain socioeconomic advantages. His affirmation of the civil equality of each member of the state as a subject indeed leads him also to advocate the equal distribution of the opportunity to rise in the social hierarchy independently of considerations of social origin.

The fact that Kant subscribes to a principle of egalitarian distributive justice does, however, not preclude his leaving untouched a considerable number of socioeconomic inequalities. As we have just seen, he does not recommend, as contemporary luck egalitarians do, the neutralization of the effects of good or bad luck on a person's access to advantaged social positions. To this, we can add that he does not evoke any duty to equalize the 'playing field' either, that is, to ensure that everyone has at least a fair chance to acquire the qualifications required to occupy a higher social position (through a public education, for instance). Thus, when he claims that everyone should 'be able to rise from lower to higher offices' (MM 6: 328) or that nobody should be prevented by another 'from attaining by their own merit the higher levels of subordination' (TP 8: 293), what he means is not that all subjects should be given the means to acquire the qualifications needed for a social ascension, but rather that no subject possessing the needed qualifications should be prevented from attaining a higher social position.[11]

Importantly, Kant also openly maintains that the equality of all members of the state as subjects is compatible with 'the greatest inequality in terms of the quantity and degree of their possessions' (TP 8: 291), and does not exclude

---

[10] We will see later that the expression 'distributive justice' has for Kant a different meaning than the one that prevails today.

[11] As we will see further on, some commentators think however that Kant's political philosophy allows for a substantive reading of the principle of equality of opportunity, which points to a duty to promote (and not only not to prevent) social mobility.

relations of 'dependence upon the will of others' either (MM 6: 315). Even if Kant is opposed to the inheritance of a 'rank' and its related legal advantages, he is not opposed to the inheritance of all things that can be acquired and alienated as a property (TP 8: 293). He also admits that the inheritance of things can generate important inequalities of wealth, and thereby, relations of economic dependence between subjects. He recalls in this context how much the welfare of the poor may depend on the will of the rich (TP 8: 292). But he also mentions the situation of all those who, in order to survive, must serve and be paid by others (this is the case for day labourers and domestic servants, for instance) (TP 8: 291). More fundamentally, it is important to emphasize that even if Kant is opposed to the idea that a rank or a legal advantage may be inherited, he is not opposed to the idea that they may legitimately exist. As he indicates in *On the common saying*, the equality of each member of the state as a subject is perfectly compatible with the greatest inequality in terms of 'rights generally (of which there can be many) relatively to others' (TP 8: 291). There is, for instance, no violation of civil equality when a rank is attached to an office (the rank of a higher magistracy, for instance) because the subject is in this case expected to perform special services (MM 6: 328), and because the day when they will leave the office, they will also leave the rank attached to the office and return among the people (TPP 8: 351). More controversially, Kant also argues that subjects are not equal before the right to vote: excluded are not only children and women, but also all those who must hire their labour or 'giv[e] others permission to make use of [their] powers' (TP 8: 295) in order to obtain their means of subsistence and hence to maintain their existence, the reason being that 'they have to be under the direction or protection of other individuals' and therefore possess no civil independence (TP 8: 295; MM 6: 313–5). Only those subjects who '*serve[]* no one other than the commonwealth' qualify for the right to vote or for active citizenship (TP 8: 295).

Kant's discussion of those workers who lack civil independence is troubling because it illustrates the way in which inequalities of possessions can lead to relations of dependence, which can in turn lead to inequalities of political rights. To be sure, Kant mentions two conditions that must be met in order for their situation to be conform to right. The first is that their dependence may not be absolute. Workers cannot, by a rightful deed, bind themselves to such a dependence that they cease to be a person and become a thing whose force can be used by another at their discretion (TP 8: 293; MM 6: 283; MM 6: 330). Labour contracts must be concluded 'only for an unspecified time, within which one party may give the other notice' (MM 6: 283) and 'only for work that is determined as to its kind and its amount' (MM 6: 330). The second condition is that their dependence may not be frozen in time or be considered innate. Workers may not be condemned to remain forever at the service of other individuals, but must be able to attain a condition of civil independence independently of their social origin. Still, it remains that any inequalities that subsist between these workers and those who enjoy civil independence after these two conditions have been met do not seem to have to be combatted as a matter of right. Nothing in Kant indicates that it is contrary to right for a worker to oblige themselves, through a contract, to serve another in exchange for wage, food, or protection, not even if they depend on this relation of dependence for the maintenance of their existence and are as a result deprived of the right to vote.

This claim may seem to contradict Kant's inclusion of civil independence among the attributes inseparable from the essence of a citizen. This inclusion could indeed be taken to mean that civil independence must be *realized* by all members of society and that, therefore, any form of civil dependence must be considered unjust and be eliminated. A view of this kind is held by Sarah Holtman, who claims that in order to determine what Kantian justice requires, we must take up the perspective of persons who enjoy civil independence – i.e., who are self-governing as much in their voting behaviour as in their development of a long-term life plan – and who infers from this the existence of a duty of right to 'meaningfully acknowledge and seek to promote the independence of individual citizens' (Holtman 2004: 88). One may also mention Jacob Weinrib, who arrives at a similar conclusion, though by a slightly different route. He thus argues that the state has a duty to establish the conditions of universal independence, but also adds that it acquires this duty because it creates and solidifies relations of civil dependence, which conflict with the idea of the original contract (Weinrib 2008: 18–21).

These views are, however, difficult to reconcile with several passages of the *Doctrine of right*. A first thing to note is, indeed, that Kant explicitly acknowledges the validity of a contract of '*letting of work* on hire' (*Lohnvertrag*), where a worker allows another to make use of their powers for a specified price (MM 6: 285) and nowhere indicates that this validity can be affected by the fact that this worker depends on the hiring of their labour for their survival. He goes even further since his discussion of the 'right of a head of the household' reveals that he also acknowledges the validity of a contract by which a servant 'agrees *to do whatever is permissible* for the welfare of the household' (MM 6: 360), and even also places themselves in the belongings of a head of the household (in the sense that the head of the household can˙bring them back under control unilaterally if they run away (MM 6: 283).[12] Last but not least, talking specifically of persons lacking civil independence, he clearly and unambiguously claims

---

[12] It must be noted that this discussion is not restricted to some scattered marginal remarks, but is embedded in a larger section devoted to the 'rights to persons akin to rights to things', which Kant takes to constitute the third branch of acquired right and to which, aware of its controversial

that '[t]his dependence upon the will of others and this inequality is, however, in no way opposed to their freedom and equality *as human beings*, who together make up a people' (MM 6: 315). Far from condemning public laws admitting a status of civil dependence, these different passages indicate that it is perfectly possible for these laws to be conform to right and hence to gain the consent of a whole people.

I suggest that the most sensible way of accounting for this 'possible consent', and correlatively, for the compatibility of civil dependence with the attributes of the citizen, is to distinguish between two ways in which public laws can agree with civil independence and to argue that Kantian justice requires *not to destroy or prevent* civil independence (a negative agreement), but not to *promote* it (a positive agreement).[13] This way of proceeding finds support in the care with which Kant distinguishes valid labour contracts from slavery contracts. Slavery contracts are contrary to right because they imply the destruction of freedom, and with it, of independence. A person obliges themselves to such a dependence that they cease to be a person and hence to have any obligation to respect a contract, which is self-contradictory and contrary to the right of humanity in their own person. By contrast, it is entirely possible for contracts of let and hire to be conform to right, and hence to gain the consent of a whole people, because, even if they fail to promote civil independence, they do not destroy or prevent it either. The artisan or the day labourer who is hired for a job that is specified as to its kind and its amount, does not make themselves into the property of another since they do not authorize another to use their powers at their discretion (MM 6: 330). Likewise, what the servant places in the belongings of the head of the household is not property in their person, but only 'usufruct': they authorize the head of the household to make use of their person as a means to their end, but not to infringe upon their personality (MM 6: 359).

The contrast that Kant establishes between these different kinds of contracts indicates that when he presents the attributes of the citizen as the principles on which all rightful legislation of a people must be based (TPP 8: 349–50), what he basically means is that there are moral limits to what a citizen may

---

nature, he provides further details in an Appendix in order to 'clarif[y] and defen[d] . . . a strange type of right which has recently been added to the doctrine on natural law, although it has always been tacitly in use' (MM 6: 361).

[13] A parallel can be drawn here with the two ways in which a maxim can agree with humanity as an end in itself, namely negatively by not conflicting with it and positively by harmonizing with it (G 4: 430). This parallel also suggests that the promotion of civil independence is a matter of beneficence rather than justice, which does not mean that the promotion of civil independence is unrelated to justice. Beneficence could indeed be regarded as serving the cause of justice. Such a view is endorsed by O'Neill, who argues that a justice-based commitment not to coerce or to deceive others involves a beneficence-based commitment to empowering the powerless and making them less dependent on others (O'Neill 2000: 137–42).

voluntarily consent to. Civil freedom, equality, and independence refer not so much to what subjects should become or realize as to what citizens are not morally authorized to renounce when making laws. Independence is innate in the sense that no contract is required to become one's own master (it is sufficient to attain the ability to support oneself), but also in the sense that any status of civil dependence between free persons can only be established through a contract, and there are moral limits on what can be contracted upon (MM 6: 282–3; MM 6: 360). If the attribute of civil independence must be taken as a reference point, it is not in the sense that public laws ought to promote it and to be considered unjust if they fail to do so, but in the sense that public laws may not contradict it and prevent a subject, in a coercive way, from rising from a passive to an active condition – by maintaining them, for instance, eternally in a condition of civil dependence because of their social origin. Kantian justice requires the abolition of formal barriers to civil independence, but it does not require the abolition of all forms of civil dependence.

It is also important to note that the principle of formal equality of opportunity does not exhaust Kant's account of socioeconomic justice at the domestic level. As we will see now, Kant indeed also recognizes the existence of a duty of right to alleviate poverty, and more precisely, to provide assistance to those members of society who are unable to maintain their existence on their own, notably through their labour and property.

3.4 A Duty of Right to Combat Poverty

There are several reasons to think that Kant does not regard poverty as a problem of right or justice. To begin with, he explicitly affirms that the concept of right has nothing to do with the satisfaction of needs. As he indicates at the beginning of the *Introduction to the doctrine of right*, right does not concern 'the relation of one's choice to the mere wish (hence also to the mere need) of the other, as in actions of beneficence' (MM 6: 230). Right does not purport to promote the happiness of human beings, not even to satisfy their basic needs, but rather to protect their external freedoms or freedoms of action in accordance with universal laws. As Kant points out, human beings could be much happier without a republican state securing their rights – as in the state of nature, by enjoying a lawless freedom, or as in a despotic state, by exchanging their freedom for an increase in material well-being (MM 6: 318). Kant also repeatedly affirms that happiness could not constitute an appropriate basis for an external lawgiving (G 4: 418; TP 8: 289–90; TP 8: 298). The ideas that human beings develop about their happiness are so imprecise, changing, and diverse that no universally valid principle could be deduced from them. Any pretention to universality in this domain is in fact a mere generalization on the basis of experience – a generalization to which we would continuously be obliged to recognize exceptions if we want to avoid violating individuals' right to pursue their own conception of happiness.

And yet, in a passage of the *Doctrine of right*, Kant grants the state the right to levy taxes for the poor and hence to redistribute wealth in a coercive way. Given the importance of this passage in terms of poverty relief and the fact that it seems to call into question what has just been said, it deserves to be quoted in its entirety:

> To the supreme commander there belongs *indirectly*, that is, insofar as he has taken over the duty of the people, the right to impose taxes on the people for its own preservation, such as taxes to support organizations providing for the *poor, foundling homes*, and *church organizations*, usually called charitable or pious institutions. The general will of the people has united itself into a society which is to maintain itself perpetually; and for this end it has submitted itself to the internal authority of the state in order to maintain those members of the society who are unable to maintain themselves. For reasons of state the government is therefore authorized to constrain the wealthy to provide the means of sustenance to those who are unable to provide for even their most necessary natural needs. The wealthy have acquired an obligation to the commonwealth, since they owe their existence to an act of submitting to its protection and care, which they need in order to live; on this obligation the state now bases its right to contribute what is theirs to maintaining their fellow citizens. (MM 6: 325–6)

Before proceeding to the interpretation of this passage, three remarks are in order. First, this passage does not evoke the existence of a right to subsistence that could be claimed by the poor, but only refers to the right to impose taxes, which indirectly pertains to the state, insofar as it is in charge of a duty that is initially incumbent on the people. Second, those who must be assisted are not the poor as such, but those who are unable to maintain themselves. This category includes foundlings, but also excludes the poor who are able to maintain themselves but fail to do so. As Kant explains a little later, poverty should not become 'a means of acquisition for the lazy', otherwise the provision of assistance would turn into an unjust burden for the people (MM 6: 326). Third, Kant specifies at the end of the quoted passage that the duty to maintain those who are unable to maintain themselves is an obligation that rich members of society have 'acquired'. This specification makes it difficult to identify the duty which the state has taken over and on which its right to impose taxes is based with a basic duty of beneficence.[14] It rather seems to refer to an obligation

---

[14] For an interpretation in terms of the duty of benevolence, see: Allen D. Rosen (1993: 179–81, 198–202)

that certain persons acquire in virtue of the specific situation in which they find themselves, *in addition to* the basic duty of beneficence they already possess simply in virtue of their humanity. The key question is then to determine in virtue of which aspect(s) of their situation they acquire this special enforceable obligation.

Two distinct, but complementary interpretations present themselves. The first, which dominates the first part of the quoted passage, refers to a duty of self-preservation on the part of the people. Kant tells us here that the general will of the people has united itself into a society that is to maintain itself perpetually and has, to this end, submitted to the power of the state, in order to maintain those members of society who are unable to maintain themselves. This claim is somewhat reminiscent of a passage found in *On the common saying*, where Kant recognizes a specific case in which the state can legitimately legislate with a view to prosperity, namely when it deems it necessary for the preservation of the commonwealth (TP 8: 298–9). To be sure, prosperity is not the 'end' of the institution of a state or civil constitution. But it can be pursued as a 'means' to give the people the strength to resist internal or external threats, and in this way, to protect a rightful condition. As Kant puts it, the head of state does not have 'to make the people happy against its will but only to make it exist as a commonwealth' (ibid.). It could be objected that a commonwealth or a society could very well maintain itself without each of its individual members being maintained. The fact, for instance, that a commonwealth or a society lets part of its population starve does not imply its own dissolution as a commonwealth or as a society. However, this objection neglects the normative dimension Kant attributes to the state. To begin with, the state or civil union – which '*is* not so much a society but rather *makes* one' (MM 6: 307) – differs from all other kinds of unions that human beings can form in that it is the only union that is in itself an end, that is, an end that they 'ought to have' (TP 8: 289). The institution of the state is a moral duty, which means that the state, as well as the society that it makes, ought to exist and ought to do so not in a temporary, but in a perpetual way. Moreover, as we have seen, the institution of the state must be understood through the idea of the original contract. The *a priori* principles of freedom, equality, and independence 'are not so much laws given by a state already established as rather principles in accordance with which alone the establishment of a state is possible in conformity with pure rational principles of external human right' (TP 8: 290). There is no doubt that a society could, as a matter of fact, very well subsist with a reduced population, just as there is no doubt that the public laws of the state could, as a matter of fact, completely neglect the plight of those who, among its members, are not able to maintain themselves. But if we are to take seriously the idea that the institution of a state must be thought and assessed in light of the idea of the original contract, then this must have implications in terms of the preservation of its individual members.

These implications become particularly apparent when we look at Kant's theory of property. Kant takes the view that in order for a person to be able to set and pursue their own ends, and hence to exercise their external freedom, it is not enough that they have the right to use external objects, but they must also have the right to exclude others from the use of external objects that are not in that person's own physical possession. In other words, a person must be able to enjoy property rights and not only use rights over external objects. If it were impossible to have an external object as one's own, external freedom would contradict itself because it 'would be depriving itself of the use of its choice with regard to an object of choice' (MM 6: 250). However, a person cannot by a simple act of choice (as a first taking into possession) impose on others an obligation that they would otherwise not have – namely, an obligation to refrain from using an external object that no one is physically using – because this would amount to limiting their freedom in a unilateral way and hence to contradicting the idea of external freedoms coexisting in accordance with universal laws. There can be agreement with their external freedoms only if there is a guarantee of reciprocity: the unilateral will must give way to an omnilateral will or a will of all. Each person must submit to the same obligation they impose on others, which is only possible if all submit to coercive public laws, and hence, if all enter a '*rightful condition, under an authority giving laws publicly, that is, ... a civil condition*' (MM 6: 255). The civil condition or the state thus appears as the precondition of property rights. In addition, all members of the state must be able to consent to the public laws that govern them, otherwise these laws could not possibly be regarded as the fruit of their united omnilateral will and hence be in conformity with right.

The right of the state to impose redistributive taxes on the rich can be understood in light of this requirement of reciprocity. A whole people could not possibly consent to property laws that leave certain subjects unable to preserve their existence since, as we have seen, a human being is not morally authorized to renounce their freedom by a contract, and by renouncing the possibility of preserving their existence, they would also renounce their freedom. In order for property laws to accord with right, they must be complemented by an aid of the state in favour of those members of society they leave unable to survive by themselves – notably those they leave both incapable of 'having some *property* (and any art, craft, fine art, or science can be counted as property) that supports [them]' (TP 8: 295) and incapable of obtaining the means of subsistence by hiring their services.

One could retort that the right to freedom requires not only that people be able to preserve their existence, but also that they not be forced to 'be under the direction or protection of other individuals' (MM 6: 315). Noteworthy, this view lies in the background of many contemporary interpretations of the Kantian problem of poverty (Hasan 2018; Ripstein 2009: 267–86; Varden 2006; Weinrib 2008). While these interpretations diverge in important respects, they all mobilize the idea that if poverty must be combatted by the Kantian state, it is in the last instance because it involves a form of freedom-threatening and hence unjust dependence.

However, these dependence-based interpretations encounter two difficulties. The first is that a freedom-threatening relation of dependence can exist between persons whose survival is not at stake; yet, Kant's defence of the state's duty to redistribute wealth revolves exclusively around ideas of being able to maintain oneself, 'means of sustenance' and 'most necessary natural needs' (MM 6: 325–6). The second difficulty is that, as we have seen, even those labour relations where dependence is most complete – i.e., where a person depends on the hiring of their services for their very survival – are not regarded by Kant as necessarily contrary to right.

Here again, it seems appropriate to introduce a distinction between *not destroying* and *promoting* freedom. Since human beings are not morally authorized to renounce their freedom by a contract, they could not possibly consent to public laws that leave them incapable of maintaining their existence – their existence being a precondition of their freedom. The duty of right to always affirm oneself as an end in relation to others presupposes a duty of right not to reduce oneself to a mere means to ensure the existence and *a fortiori* the flourishing of others. By consenting to property laws that prevent their survival, and hence the very freedom that gives these laws their raison d'être, human beings consent to ceasing being persons and contradict the 'right of humanity in their own person'.[15]

In addition to avoiding the previously mentioned difficulties, the interpretation proposed here also allows us to make sense of Kant's claim that only those

---

[15] Among contemporary commentators who escape the difficulties encountered by dependence-based approaches to the Kantian problem of poverty, one can mention Paul Guyer (2000: ch. 7). His approach is close to the one adopted here in that it also revolves around the idea that a system of property cannot be just unless it can gain the consent of all those it affects. But Guyer understands this requirement of 'possible consent' differently since he integrates in it considerations of rational interest, and argues that it will be in the interest of a person to consent to a system of property only if this system provides them an opportunity to maintain their existence that is equivalent to that they would enjoy without this system. The interpretation defended here has the advantage of avoiding counterfactual comparisons involving considerations of self-interest to concentrate on what a person is morally authorized to consent to given the 'right of humanity in their own person'.

poor who, just like foundlings, are unable to obtain the means of subsistence by themselves ought as a matter of right to be assisted by their fellow citizens. Those who could maintain their existence by selling their property or by hiring their services, but who, out of laziness or for some other reason, prefer to rely on others to obtain what they need to survive are explicitly excluded from the scope of the duty of right to assist the poor. That is, not all those who lack civil independence ought to be helped by the state as a matter of right.

A second interpretation, which is based on the last sentence of the previously quoted passage, appeals to considerations of fair return. Kant claims not only that the people have the duty to maintain those members of society who are unable to maintain themselves, but also, and more particularly, that it is the 'wealthy' who have 'acquired' this duty because 'they owe their existence to an act of submitting to [the] protection and care [of the commonwealth], which they need in order to live'. The duty to redistribute wealth seems here to take on the traits of a duty of fair return: this duty is owed by the wealthy, and the reason the wealthy are identified as the bearers of this duty is not simply that they are wealthy or have 'abundant means for the happiness of others, i.e., means in excess of [their] own needs' (MM 6: 453), but also that they owe their lives, and *a fortiori* their wealth, to the existence of the commonwealth.

There are traces of this interpretation further in the *Doctrine of right*, in a passage of the 'Right of nations' that asks whether the state has the right to use its subjects for war on the ground that it has in some way 'made' them and that one has 'the right to do what one wants with what belongs to one (one's property)' (MM 6: 344–5). As can be expected, Kant answers in the negative: the state may not use, exploit, or kill its subjects as if they were its property, but must always consider them as 'colegislating members of a state'. However, and this is the relevant point for our discussion, Kant also acknowledges that human beings are to a certain extent the 'product' of their state because without a government securing their acquisitions and possessions, a country would not have yielded abundant natural products, and as a consequence, would not have allowed many people to come into existence and to survive either (MM 6: 345). This passage offers illuminating insights into the reason why the wealthy can be said to owe their existence to the commonwealth. It points out that if they have been able to acquire their wealth and even to maintain their existence, it is not only because of their talents or industriousness (i.e., their merit), but also because public laws securing their acquisitions and possessions have been established and because all members of society have limited their freedom of action accordingly. Even if this contribution by the state and its members does not authorize the state to treat the wealthy as if they were its property or as a mere means, it authorizes and even requires it to force them to contribute to the preservation of those members of society who, in spite of existing public laws, remain unable to maintain themselves. It is in fact the latter who, without aid, would be used as mere means to promote the enrichment and, more broadly, the ends of other members of society.

This detour through Kant's conception of domestic distributive justice has been a necessary step to take before addressing the issue of global distributive justice. It has allowed us to identify two types of socioeconomic inequalities that can, according to Kant, be attributed to the injustice of the government: those based on the formal recognition of innate privileges and those involving an incapacity to maintain one's existence. It has also shown us that these inequalities must be tackled by reforming existing domestic public laws, and more precisely, by implementing two domestic principles of socioeconomic or distributive justice: a principle of formal equality of opportunity and a principle of wealth redistribution in favour of those members of society who are unable to maintain their existence. These two principles of justice give us an indication of the double direction that our reflection will have to take at the global level, namely, 'Can a global principle of formal equality of opportunity be invoked to condemn certain forms of global inequalities?' and 'Can rich states be said to have a duty of right to relieve global poverty?' But before determining whether the arguments Kant offers in favour of domestic duties of right to combat certain forms of poverty and inequality can be extended beyond the state, we must address another, logically prior question. This question, which is certainly one of the most hotly debated questions among contemporary global justice thinkers, is the question of the 'circumstances of distributive justice': Do principles of distributive justice, whatever the conception of distributive justice one endorses, apply between all human beings simply by virtue of their humanity or do they only apply between human beings who are together involved in certain kinds of institutional configurations, and if so, which ones?

3.5 The Circumstances of Distributive Justice

The question of the circumstances of distributive justice is admittedly not new, but it came back to the forefront after the publication of John Rawls's *A Theory of Justice* (1971), and once again, after the publication of Rawls's *The Law of Peoples* (1999). In the field of global justice, this renewed interest was prompted by Rawls's explicit refusal to extend the scope of the principles of egalitarian distributive justice that he advocates in the domestic sphere – namely, a principle of fair equality of opportunity and a difference principle[16] – to the

---

[16] Thus, Rawls tells us that, in the domestic sphere, '[s]ocial and economic inequalities are to satisfy two conditions: first, they are to be attached to offices and positions open to all under conditions of fair equality of opportunity; and second, they are to be to the greatest benefit of the least-advantaged members of society (the difference principle)' (Rawls 2001: 42–3).

global sphere. In the latter case, he favours instead a 'duty of assistance', which he defines as 'a duty to assist other peoples living under unfavourable conditions that prevent their having a just or decent political and social regime' (Rawls 1999: 37). Rawls's refusal to recognize duties of global egalitarian distributive justice is the sign that he conceives of such duties as special duties, which are activated only when certain conditions obtain. Rawls does not elaborate on the reasons why, according to him, these conditions are not met in the global sphere. When discussing the proposal made by Charles Beitz in favour of a global principle of distribution, he only mentions: 'He believes that in this case [when there are flows of trade and services between countries] a global system of cooperation already exists' (Rawls 1999: 116).

It thus comes as no surprise that many commentators have attempted to identify and explicate the factors which, from a Rawlsian perspective, justify the application of egalitarian distributive justice within but not outside the state. Two main interpretations have emerged. The first makes the application of egalitarian distributive requirements conditional on the existence of a certain kind of cooperative venture (e.g., Freeman 2007: ch. 8; Sangiovanni 2007). Proponents of this interpretation do not deny the existence of international cooperation, but in their view, international cooperation is of a fundamentally different kind than domestic social cooperation and need, as such, not satisfy egalitarian distributive requirements in order to be morally acceptable. The second interpretation makes, for its part, the application of egalitarian distributive requirements conditional on the existence of certain forms of coercion or non-voluntariness (e.g., Blake 2001; Nagel 2005; Reidy 2007). Proponents of this interpretation deny that the international sphere comprises a coercive structure of the relevant sort and tend to present international institutions as associations which have been established on a voluntary basis by states and which need, therefore, not satisfy egalitarian distributive requirements in order to be morally acceptable.

The key to address the question of the circumstances of distributive justice from a Kantian point of view is provided by the 'postulate of public right'. This postulate holds that 'when you cannot avoid living side by side with all others, you ought to leave the state of nature and proceed with them into a rightful condition, that is, a condition of distributive justice' (MM 6: 307). The equivalence that Kant establishes here between a rightful condition and a condition of distributive justice may initially surprise, but it is easily explained by the fact that Kant attributes to the expression 'distributive justice' a meaning that is different from the one that prevails today.[17] The expression, for him, does not

---

[17] The postulate of public right also appears in *Toward perpetual peace* in the following formulation: 'all men who can mutually affect one another must belong to some civil constitution' (TPP 8: 349). Its link with Kant's understanding of distributive justice is made particularly explicit in

refer to a criterion allowing us to assess the moral quality of existing public laws (such as the fairness of the way in which they distribute socioeconomic advantages, for instance), but to the very existence of public laws. A condition of distributive justice is a condition – and even the sole condition – in which everyone can '*enjoy* his rights' (MM 6: 305–6), and more specifically, in which 'what is to be recognized as belonging to it is determined *by law* and is allotted to it by adequate *power*' (MM 6: 312).

At the heart of the postulate of public right, we find a moral duty to enter a condition of distributive justice, and this duty can be deduced *a priori*, by contrasting the idea of the rightful condition with that of the non-rightful condition. Given that the non-rightful condition (or the state of nature) is by definition devoid of external laws, it does not allow agents to resolve their disputes in a 'civil' way, that is, by means of a decision pronounced by a competent judge and having as a result rightful force (MM 6: 312–3). Even if agents do not wrong each other *de facto* – even if, for instance, they do not actually attack or deceive each other – and even if they are 'well disposed and law-abiding' (MM 6: 312), the non-rightful condition remains a condition '*devoid of justice* (*status iustitia vacuus*)' (ibid.), in which the only way to defend one's right when one believes to be wronged by another is the 'barbaric way', that is, the use of force (MM 6: 351). This explains why the non-rightful condition is also characterized as being a 'condition of war', in which the 'right of the stronger' prevails (MM 6: 344). Yet, as we have seen, right can only be determined by external laws that hold universally and that equally limit the external freedom of each, never by unilateral maxims and hence by violence: 'reason, from the throne of the highest morally legislative power, delivers an absolute condemnation of war as a procedure for determining rights' (TPP 8: 356). This is why all agents who can affect each other by their external actions have the moral duty to leave the state of nature and to enter a rightful condition or a condition of distributive justice. And as Kant emphasizes, this duty holds as much between individuals as between states, and also between individuals and foreign states (TPP 8: 349; MM 6: 311). That is, the postulate of public right demands not only that we enter a domestic rightful condition, but also that we enter an interstate and even a cosmopolitan rightful condition.

To come back to the question of the circumstances of distributive justice, the important thing that the postulate of public right reveals to us is that it is not enough to point to the voluntary character or even to the absence of certain institutional configurations on a global scale to infer the absence of any duties of

---

the *Introduction to the doctrine of right*, where the Ulpian formula '*suum cuique tribue*' is connected with the following duty of right: '(If you cannot help associating with others), *enter* into a society with them in which each can keep what is his' (MM 6: 237).

global distributive justice (in the contemporary or socioeconomic sense of the term). To begin with, the fact that it is on a voluntary basis that human beings or states have agreed to subject themselves to external laws does not in any way exempt them from the duty to continuously reform these laws in order to get them closer to the idea of the original contract. It is the latter requirement, and not the non-voluntariness of existing institutions, which involves a duty to combat certain forms of poverty and socioeconomic inequality. Moreover, and even more important, the very absence of certain institutional configurations can be contrary to right. It can, for instance, result from the willingness of the strongest to remain in a non-rightful condition and to take advantage of their position of superiority to unilaterally impose their decisions on the weakest. Yet, the Kantian postulate of public right entails that by so acting they 'do wrong in the highest degree' (MM 6: 307) because 'they take away any validity from the concept of right itself and hand everything over to savage violence, as if by law, and so subvert the right of human beings as such' (MM 6: 308). Making the application of duties of distributive justice (in the contemporary socioeconomic sense of the term) conditional on the previous existence of certain institutional configurations can even lead to moral aberrations. More particularly, it can lead to the weakest being doubly disadvantaged: first, by the absence of external laws governing their interaction with the strongest, laws in the absence of which no justice is possible; second, by the absence of any duty to reform existing external laws so as to ensure that no one is prevented from maintaining their existence and from raising themselves to a higher social position.[18]

Assuming that the Kantian 'circumstances of distributive justice' obtain whenever agents can affect each other through their external actions, the main question to be elucidated is not whether these circumstances obtain in the global sphere. As we have just seen, Kant explicitly recognizes that there is a duty to enter an interstate and a cosmopolitan rightful condition. The key question is rather whether the duty of global distributive justice in the Kantian sense of the term also implies a duty of global distributive justice in the contemporary or socioeconomic sense of the term, that is, whether the duty to enter a rightful condition beyond the state also implies a duty to combat certain forms of global socioeconomic inequalities. It is to this question that we now turn.

4 Justice in the Face of Global Poverty and Inequality

This section explores in more detail the distributive implications that the postulate of public right may have on a global scale. More particularly, it

---

[18] For similar concerns, related to the specific claim that demands of distributive justice are activated only by the coercive apparatus of the state, see: Ryan Pevnick (2008: 404–6).

addresses the following two questions: 'Can rich states be said to have a duty of right to relieve global poverty?' and 'Can a global principle of formal equality of opportunity be invoked to condemn certain forms of global inequalities?' The first part focuses on the subject-matter of interstate public right, namely, the protection of the *mine or yours* of states. It starts by clarifying the content of the mine or yours of states and then brings into relief the complex nature of the Kantian duty to enter a rightful condition, which comprises both a conservative and an ideal dimension. The second part examines whether and to what extent the arguments Kant offers in favour of domestic duties of right to combat certain forms of poverty and inequality can be extended from the domestic to the global sphere. The reflection moves here beyond the scope of interstate public right to consider Kant's theory of cosmopolitan right and its bearing on issues of transnational mobility of persons and goods.

4.1 A Rightful Condition beyond the State

Kant's theory of interstate right provides a good starting point for addressing the question of global distributive justice. Even though it leads us to restrict our attention to a specific type of global actor and to consider, for instance, the duties of rich states rather than those of the global rich in general (rich individuals can indeed also be found within poor states and vice versa), it comprises Kant's most elaborate exposition of what a rightful condition could mean beyond the state. Importantly, it also teaches us that human beings are not the only entities to which Kant attributes a moral personality: states too are depicted as 'moral persons', endowed with rights and duties, including a duty to enter a rightful condition. This foreshadows the need to balance the rights possessed by different types of global actors (states versus individuals, for instance), which lies at the heart of Kant's theory of cosmopolitan right.

As already indicated, Kant argues that both individuals and states, insofar as they can affect each other through their external actions, have a moral duty to enter a rightful condition understood as a condition governed by external laws. It is also in these terms that he conceives of distributive justice since, in his view, the rightful condition is nothing else than a condition of distributive justice. To be sure, Kant acknowledges important differences between the interindividual and the interstate situations, especially in terms of coercion. While individuals have the right to coerce each other to enter a rightful condition, states, he argues, escape this coercion. As he puts it,

> [W]hat holds in accordance with natural right for human beings in a lawless condition, "they ought to leave this condition", cannot hold for states in accordance with the right of nations (since, as states, they already have

a rightful constitution internally and hence have outgrown the constraint of others to bring them under a more extended law-governed constitution in accordance with their concepts of right). (MM 8: 355–6)

According to this passage, an important difference between the interindividual and the interstate states of nature is that the latter is not completely devoid of right. Since it is by definition made up of states, the interstate state of nature is characterized by the coexistence of multiple domestic rightful conditions. If a state could rightfully be coerced by other states to enter an enlarged civil constitution, it would not only risk being submitted to a constitution that is less just than the one it already possesses (Laberge 1998: 93), but it would also, and more radically, risk having its rightful condition dissolved into the meanders of an international conflict or civil war. Yet, as Kant emphasizes, 'some rightful constitution or other, even if it is only to a small degree in conformity with right, is better than none at all' (TPP 8: 373). The interstate rightful condition must therefore be established not by force, but through a voluntary alliance between states, which neighbouring states are able to join and which can gradually extend to the whole world (TPP 8: 356).

Still, even if this point of divergence indicates that the interstate situation cannot be seen as a mere replica of the interindividual situation on a larger scale, it is important to note that the subject-matter of public right remains considerably similar in both cases, namely, the protection of what belongs to each. What belongs to each divides in Kant into an 'innate right' or right that is possessed by nature (*the internal mine or yours*) and an 'acquired right' or right whose acquisition requires a rightful deed (*the external mine or yours*) (MM 6: 237). As far as individuals are concerned, Kant tells us that '*There is only one innate right*', namely, '*Freedom* (independence from being constrained by another's choice), insofar as it can coexist with the freedom of every other in accordance with a universal law' (MM 6: 237). Their acquired rights can, for their part, relate to a corporeal thing external to them (property right), to another's choice to perform a specific deed (contract right) or to another's status in relation to them (rights to persons akin to rights to things) (MM 6: 248). In an analogous way, the innate right of states can be seen as referring to their right to political independence and their acquired rights as covering essentially their territorial possessions and the agreements they have concluded with others. Kant indeed conceives of states as 'moral persons' (MM 6: 343; TPP 8: 344) which, just like human beings (and unlike things), are subject to the laws of freedom or moral laws and whose actions can as a consequence be imputed to them (MM 6: 223; Byrd 1995: 172). States are free in the sense that they have the capacity to set themselves ends or to act on rational principles (i.e., the capacity of self-determination). And insofar as they are free, they also have certain duties and rights – notably, a duty not to interfere with the internal affairs of other states and a right not to depend on the constraining choice of another insofar as this right can coexist with the same right of all others in accordance with universal laws. This innate right to independence is also an innate right to equality since it excludes certain states being by nature destined to command or to obey other states. As Kant puts it, the relation of states to each other is not the relation of a superior (*imperantis*) to those subject to him (*subditum*) (MM 6: 347).

Admittedly, the mine or yours of states has its own specific characteristics. One of them is that, unlike individuals, states seem inconceivable without the possession of a well-defined territory. This has led Arthur Ripstein to argue that the relation of a state to its territory is for Kant similar to the relation of an individual to their body, and that the territory of a state must therefore be regarded as belonging to the innate (and not acquired) right of that state (Ripstein 2009: 227–8).

Yet, we find in Kant's work several passages that identify the territory of a state with a property, and hence with an external mine or yours. Thus, when talking about the state of nature, Kant tells us in *On the common saying* that 'No state is for a moment secure from others in either its independence [*Selbständigkeit*] or its property. The will to subjugate one another or to diminish what belongs to another always exists' (TP 8: 312). Similarly, in *Toward perpetual peace*, he distinguishes between a state and its territory by equating the former with a moral person and the latter with a belonging or a thing:

> [A] state is not (like the land on which it resides) a belonging *(patrimonium)*. It is a society of human beings that no one other than itself can command or dispose of. Like a trunk, it has its own roots; and to annex it to another state as a graft is to do away with its existence as a moral person and to make a moral person into a thing, and so to contradict the idea of the original contract, apart from which no right over a people can be thought. (TPP 8: 344)

While the state must always be regarded as a moral person, capable of consenting to the external actions or laws that affect it, the territory it occupies must rather be seen as a belonging that can be acquired or lost. It is once again this distinction between the state as a moral person and its territory as a property that underlies Kant's claim, in the *Doctrine of right*, that the sovereign is not only the supreme commander of the people, but also the supreme proprietor of the land (MM 6: 323). Thus, even if we admit that the territory of a state is not located outside the state and seems in this sense 'attached' to the state in the same way as a body is attached to the individual it embodies, we must acknowledge that it remains different from the state and must therefore be regarded as belonging to its external or acquired right.

The claim that the territory of a state is to be regarded as belonging to the external rather than to the internal mine or yours of states is not only a terminological point. It has important normative implications since it raises the question of the just acquisition and possession of a territory. Unlike the possession of a body by an individual, the possession of a territory by a state permanently removes a given geographical space from what can be called the global commons. A state claiming a territory is claiming the right to impose on others an obligation not to use an external object that they were previously free to use. Yet, as we have seen, such an obligation requires a guarantee of reciprocity, and more precisely, a submission to external laws conforming to the idea of the original contract. We will return to this point later.

Having examined what the rights of states consist of, let us stop for a moment to consider the nature of the Kantian duty to enter a rightful condition. As Kant specifies in the *Introduction to the doctrine of right*, the point of this duty is not to enter a condition which '[g]ives to each what is *his*' because 'one cannot give anyone something he already has', but to enter a condition 'in which what belongs to each can be secured to him against everyone else' (MM 6: 237). Similarly, when discussing interstate public right, Kant insists on the idea that the aim of this right is not to allow states to increase their political power or to acquire territory, but to prevent states from being subjugated or from losing their territory (MM 6: 347; MM 6: 349; TPP 8: 356). Its focus is on ensuring that each state can keep what is its own, namely its independence and its property.

The nature of the Kantian duty to enter a rightful condition is, however, more complex than appears at first sight. How, indeed, can public right be said to secure what belongs to each while, as we have seen in the previous section, it is also said to be the precondition of property? Is it not contradictory to claim, on the one hand, that public right must secure the property of each individual or the territory of each state, and on the other hand, that property and territorial rights must obtain the sanction of an omnilateral will and hence need public right in order to exist?

The answer to these questions is provided by the notion of 'provisional right'. Kant indeed claims that it is possible to have a '*provisionally rightful* possessions' (MM 6: 257): 'before the establishment of the civil condition but with a view to it, that is, *provisionally*, it is a *duty* to proceed in accordance with the principle of external acquisition. Accordingly, there is also a rightful *capacity* [*rechtliches Vermögen*] of the will to bind everyone to recognize the act of taking possession and of appropriation as valid, even though it is only unilateral' (MM 6: 267). As far as individuals are concerned, this rightful capacity finds its justification in the idea that the possession of property rights is necessary for the exercise of external freedom. And since individuals cannot be expected to wait until they enter a civil condition before being authorized to exercise their external freedom, they must also be authorized to have provisional property rights or provisionally rightful possessions. Importantly, Kant also adds that provisionally rightful possessions are subject to a condition: individuals are authorized to unilaterally exclude others from the use of the external objects they have been the first to take into possession and they want to be 'theirs', *provided* that they take the civil condition and its establishment as their focal point, and more particularly, provided they accord their external possessions with the 'possibility of [a civil] condition', which 'can be based only on a law of a common will' (MM 6: 257, MM 6: 264). Bringing external possessions in accord with the possibility of a civil condition involves two basic requirements of reciprocity: individuals must be willing to respect the external possessions claimed by others, and they must make sure that everyone can consent to the way in which external possessions are distributed. It is the observance of these two requirements which puts them in a position to have provisionally rightful possessions.[19]

Although this argument is developed by Kant with regard to the property rights of individuals, it may also be extended to the territorial rights of states. To begin with, Kant explicitly recognizes that it is also possible for states to have provisional external rights:

---

[19] Unlike interpretations that tend to emphasize either the conservative aspect (e.g., Byrd and Hurschka 2010: 101, 138–9) or the constitutive aspect (e.g., Flikschuh 2000: 140, 148–9; Korsgaard 2018: 29–30) of the duty to enter a rightful condition as regards property rights, the interpretation defended here centres on the necessary complementarity of both aspects. It mobilizes the notion of 'provisional rights', which it takes to be at the same time genuine rights, which can be defended by force and which others have a duty to respect, and conditional rights, whose rightfulness depends on their holders' readiness to respect others' property claims and on the capacity of the existing distribution of property to gain the consent of all those subject to it. This interpretation allows us to make sense of some seemingly contradictory passages of the *Doctrine of right*, which oscillate between the idea that the rightful condition only secures what belongs to each (MM 6: 256) and the idea that property rights are impossible without a rightful condition (MM 6: 255). This interpretation also finds an outstanding illustration in the ongoing practice of international relations: it is indeed commonly accepted that the absence of a world state does not exempt states from the duty to respect one another's (provisional) territorial rights and to ensure that the distribution of territorial rights remains morally acceptable. Last but not least, it is also in accordance with Kant's claim that property rights cannot be conclusive, but 'will always remain only provisional unless [the] contract extends to the entire human race'. (MM 6: 266) For a recent illuminating discussion on the different ways of interpreting the Kantian notion of 'provisional right', see: Hasan (2018b).

> Since a state of nature among nations, like a state of nature among individual
> human beings, is a condition that one ought to leave in order to enter a lawful
> condition, before this happens any rights of nations, and anything external
> that is mine or yours which states can acquire or retain by war, are merely
> *provisional*. Only in a universal *association of states* (analogous to that by
> which a people becomes a state) can rights come to hold *conclusively* and
> a true *condition of peace* come about. (MM 6: 350)

But one could go further and argue that in order for states to be able to set and
pursue their own ends, and hence to determine themselves, they must be able to
possess territorial rights: they must be authorized to exclude others from the use
of a well-defined geographical area, to make and enforce law on this area, and to
control both the natural resources and the borders of this area.[20] One could also
add that they must be authorized to do so before an omnilateral and powerful
will validates their territorial possessions in a conclusive way. And lastly, one
could specify that provisionally rightful territorial possessions are subject to
a condition: states must demonstrate their willingness to enter an interstate
rightful condition, and hence to accord their territorial possessions with the
possibility of a civil condition based on a law of a common will, by respecting
the territorial possessions claimed by other states and by making sure that all
states could possibly consent to the way in which territorial possessions are
distributed. What the notion of 'provisional right', whether applied to individuals or to states, thus reveals is that the Kantian duty to enter a rightful condition
has both a conservative and an ideal dimension: it is a duty to respect the
existing distribution of (property or territorial) rights while at the same time
being committed to reform it so as to bring it into conformity with rational right.

Before closing this subsection, it must be noted that, unlike most contemporary global justice thinkers, Kant identifies a third sphere of public right, which
must complement the spheres of domestic right and interstate right: the sphere
of cosmopolitan right. While one of the central issues in the contemporary
global justice debate is to determine whether global justice is to be 'interstate' or
'cosmopolitan' – that is, whether the ultimate units of moral concern at the
global level ought to be states or individuals – Kant unambiguously affirms that
it can and should be both. In his view, neither of these spheres of public right can
be reduced to the other because each of them has a fundamentally different
subject-matter. As we have just seen, interstate public right concerns the mutual
relations of states and aims to protect what belongs to each state. Cosmopolitan
right differs in that it concerns the mutual relations of states and non-state actors
(such as tribes, commercial societies, or individuals) as 'citizens of the world',

---

[20] For similar definitions of territorial rights, see: Miller (2012), Simmons (2001), Stilz (2009), and
Ypi (2014).

and aims to strike an appropriate balance in the protection of their respective rights. It aims, for instance, to secure individuals' right to try to engage in commerce with foreigners, while avoiding that the exercise of this right leads to the rights of states being violated (i.e., their right to political independence and their right to their territory). As Kant's theory of cosmopolitan right gives an important place to questions related to the transitional mobility of persons and goods, it will be of particular relevance when we address the global applicability of the principle of formal equality of opportunity.

4.2. Global Poverty and Inequality as a Matter of Right

Having examined the subject-matter and the nature of the duty to enter a rightful condition beyond the state (i.e., of the duty of global distributive justice in the Kantian sense of the term), we must now determine whether this duty also implies duties of right to combat certain forms of socioeconomic inequalities on a global scale (i.e., a duty of global distributive justice in the contemporary sense of the term). More particularly, and to come back to the questions raised at the beginning of this section: 'Can rich states be said to have a duty of right to relieve global poverty?' and 'Can a global principle of formal equality of opportunity be invoked to condemn certain forms of global inequalities?'

We cannot but admit that Kant makes no explicit reference to any duty of right to reduce global inequalities or to assist the global poor. What he does do instead is reject the existence of any right to intervene in the internal affairs of other states on the ground that the recognition of such a right 'would make the autonomy of all states insecure' (TPP 8: 346). This rejection seems to hold even when a foreign state is oppressing its own people and thus even when an intervention is invoked on humanitarian grounds. A state that forcibly interferes with the constitution and government of another state which experiences internal troubles, but which did no wrong to it, would be violating the 'right of a people dependent upon no other and only struggling with its internal illness' (ibid.).

That being said, it is important to bear in mind that when affirming the existence of a moral duty to enter a rightful condition beyond the state, Kant affirms not only the existence of a duty to submit to public laws beyond the state, but also the existence of a duty to reform these laws so as to accord them with the idea of the original contract. It is further reasonable to assume that the latter duty applies even if public right cannot be enforced on a global scale but must remain an 'unachievable idea' since, as Kant points out, the impossibility of achieving an ultimate goal does not affect the possibility of realizing the political principles that allow us to continually come closer to it (MM 6: 350).

This is in fact precisely what the notion of 'provisional right' suggests: even if the establishment of a global coercive power is highly unlikely and territorial rights are doomed to remain forever provisional, the rightful exercise of these rights requires that states accord their territorial possessions with the possibility of a civil condition based on a law of a common will, and this requirement could well have major implications in terms of global poverty and inequality.

4.2.1 A Duty of Right to Alleviate Global Poverty

As we have seen, Kant offers two complementary arguments in favour of a duty of right to relieve poverty within the state: the first is in terms of a duty of self-preservation on the part of the people, the second is in terms of a duty of fair return on the part of rich citizens. Let us start by examining the first argument: does the idea of a 'general will of the people' which 'has united itself into a society which is to maintain itself perpetually' and which has therefore 'submitted itself to the internal authority of the state in order to maintain those members of the society who are unable to maintain themselves' make sense on a global scale? For Pauline Kleingeld, the answer is negative: this argument is related to the specific structure of relations between citizens and the republic, and can therefore not fully apply on a global scale until a world republic is established (Kleingeld 2012: 146). She nonetheless suggests that the more the voluntary alliance of states will acquire the aspects of a world republic, the more it will acquire the duty to alleviate poverty (Kleingeld 2012: 147). Still, it may be doubted that Kant's first argument depends on the prior existence of a republic. As a state that conforms to the principles of rational right, the republican state represents an ideal that all actual states must strive toward. If the duty of right to assist poor states were conditional on the prior existence of a world republic, we would be confronted with the same kind of moral aberrations that affect certain conceptions of the 'circumstances of distributive justice'. Poor states would be doubly disadvantaged: first, by the absence of global institutions in conformity with right (notably, a world republic); second, by the idea that the more global institutions fail to conform to right, the less other states have a duty to assist them.

In fact, it is not even obvious that Kant's first argument depends on the prior existence of a state, republican or not. The important point is not to determine whether states can be said to form a society of a certain kind, but whether they ought to do so, and Kant's answer is unequivocal: 'A league of nations in accordance with the idea of an original social contract is necessary, not in order to meddle in one another's internal dissensions but to protect against attacks from without' (MM 6: 344). States must agree to unite their particular wills into a common will, and this will, if it is to be truly common, must pronounce public laws that could be consented to by all of them. It is also important to point out that an international public law has, as a matter of fact, already been established by states to govern their interactions and to secure their rights. The Kantian notion of provisional right reminds us that even if there is no global coercive power, states have the duty to respect the existing international public law because doing so is for them the only way to demonstrate their readiness to integrate an interstate rightful condition. Of course, the existing international public *law* can exhibit important deficiencies from the point of view of rational *right*. But the appropriate way to respond to such deficiencies is not to refuse to respect existing public laws, but rather to work peacefully on reforming these laws so as to bring them closer to the idea of the original contract.

It is at this level that the question of a duty of right to relieve global poverty must be raised. We must ask whether bringing international public laws closer to the idea of the original contract requires rich states to assist poor ones, and more specifically, whether a society of states as a whole could possibly consent to a system of territorial rights that leaves certain states unable to maintain their existence. The difficulty is of course to determine what an incapacity to maintain one's existence could mean in the case of a state. It is indeed difficult to make sense of the idea of a state that would die without aid because, however poor it may be, a state would not disappear from the surface of the earth as an individual would. I propose to overcome this difficulty by considering the most obvious reason for assisting a poor state, namely, to enable it to maintain the existence of its individual members. A state that is unable to maintain its existence would, on this reading, be a state that is unable to maintain the existence and hence the freedom of its individual members. That is to say, it would be a state that is unable to fulfil the core functions of the state, let alone to constitute itself into a republic. Yet, a society of states as a whole could not possibly consent to a system of territorial rights that leaves certain states unable to fulfil the core functions of the state. A state is indeed not morally authorized to renounce its innate right to independence and thereby its capacity to secure the freedom of its individual members. As Kant puts it in *The metaphysics of morals*, a people 'cannot lose its original right to unite itself into a commonwealth' (MM 6: 349), or again in *Toward perpetual peace*, the loss for a state of its existence as a moral person would 'contradict the idea of the original contract, apart from which no right over a people can be thought' (TPP 8: 344). In order for a system of territorial rights to accord with right, it must therefore be complemented by an aid in favour of those states that lack the resources necessary to function as independent states and to secure the lives and freedom of their individual members. As in the domestic sphere, this aid must only be provided to those agents that are unable to maintain themselves – in this case, those states that are unable to fulfil the core functions of a state, and not those states that are able but that, for some reason, do not want to do so.[21] However, the absence of a global coercive power means that this aid cannot presently be provided through redistributive taxes, but only in a voluntary way, which risks forging paternalistic relationships and hence undermining the very right to independence that the aid is aimed at securing. States might well have the duty to reform existing international public laws toward the implementation of an international system of redistributive taxes. In the meantime, one of the main challenges will be to secure the preconditions of self-determination without undermining the right to self-determination itself.

We have seen that Kant's defence of a duty of right to alleviate domestic poverty also appeals to considerations of fair return. It is because wealthy citizens owe their existence, and *a fortiori* their wealth, to the establishment of a government which secures their acquisitions and possessions, and to which all citizens are equally subject, that they ought in return, through redistributive taxes, to assist those citizens who remain unable to maintain their existence on their own. In a similar way, one could argue that wealthy states owe their existence, and *a fortiori* their wealth, to the establishment of an international public law which protects their territorial rights, and to which all states are equally subject, and that they have therefore acquired an obligation to assist those states that, in spite of the existence of international public laws, remain unable to maintain their existence on their own.

It might be objected that the main determinants of the wealth of states are not global, but domestic, and more specifically, that they have to do with factors such as 'the political culture, the political virtues and civic society of the country, its members' probity and industriousness, [and] their capacity for innovation' (Rawls 1999: 108). Or, stated slightly differently, it might be objected that even if the existing international public law protects the rights of states to and over a well-defined territory, it is above all the individual members of the state who, through their cooperation and compliance with existing domestic public laws, make it possible for the state to exist and to protect their individual rights (Sangiovanni 2007). However, a Kantian perspective reveals the shortcomings of this view. Kant indeed emphasizes the interdependence of the different spheres

---

[21] A parallel may be drawn here with Rawls, who makes it clear that '[o]nly burdened societies need help' (Rawls 1999: 106). The duty of assistance is owed only to societies which cannot establish just, or at least decent, domestic institutions because they are burdened by unfavourable historical, social, or economic circumstances, not to 'outlaw states', which refuse to comply with a reasonable Law of Peoples.

of public right. Thus, talking about the three spheres of public right that are represented by domestic right, interstate right, and cosmopolitan right, Kant affirms that 'if the principle of outer freedom limited by law is lacking in any one of these three possible forms of rightful condition, the framework of all the others is unavoidably undermined and must finally collapse' (MM 6: 311). Of particular relevance for the question that interests us here is the dependence of domestic right on interstate right. What this dependence basically means is that a domestic constitution cannot genuinely protect individuals' right to freedom unless an interstate constitution is established, which genuinely protects states' right to independence. Correlatively, individuals' property rights cannot acquire a conclusive character unless states' territorial rights are also made conclusive. It follows that no state can be regarded as owing its existence, and *a fortiori* its wealth, only to the efforts of its members or to the quality of its domestic institutions because the latter would themselves not be possible without the presence of international public laws limiting the freedom of all states, and hence without the cooperation of other states.[22]

4.2.2 A Duty of Right to Reduce Global Inequalities

This subsection takes the reflection one step further and asks whether Kant's political theory also offers reasons to be concerned with global inequalities, besides global absolute poverty. More particularly, it looks into the global applicability of Kant's principle of formal equality of opportunity. We have seen that, at the domestic level, this principle basically requires social mobility not to be hindered by arbitrary formal obstacles (such as the legal recognition of a hereditary nobility). A possible way to translate the notion of social mobility on a global scale is in terms of transnational mobility of persons. It is in this direction that Joseph Carens leads us when, questioning states' right to close their borders, he affirms that 'Citizenship in Western liberal democracies is the modern equivalent of feudal privilege – an inherited status that greatly enhances one's life chances. Like feudal birthright privileges, restrictive citizenship is hard to justify when one thinks about it closely' (Carens 1987: 252). Another way in which the notion of social mobility can be translated at the global level is in terms of transnational mobility of goods. Following Fernando Tesón, one could indeed criticize protectionist laws for 'coercively redistribut[ing] resources in favor of persons who are not deserving beneficiaries' and for 'harm[ing] the world's poor by denying them access to wealthy markets'

---

[22] In the same vein, Williams has argued that sovereigns cannot carry out their duties as supreme proprietors of the land without the cooperation of other supreme proprietors and that mutuality must therefore be fostered 'with the wealthy and poor of all nations' (Williams 2010: 71).

(Tesón 2012: 126–7). This subsection offers a cosmopolitan reading of the principle of formal equality of opportunity and raises the question of whether one could, in a Kantian spirit, conclude the injustice of public laws that hinder the transnational mobility of persons or goods on the ground that it would be impossible for 'world citizens' – that is, states, but also non-state global actors – taken as a whole to consent to such laws. This angle of approach is justified by the fact that it is essentially in passages dealing with cosmopolitan right that Kant examines the relations between different kinds of global actors and, correlatively, issues raised by transnational migration and trade.[23]

Kant's theory of cosmopolitan right hinges on the idea of the 'original possession in common of the earth'. This idea does not refer, as in the work of natural law theorists such as Hugo Grotius and Samuel Pufendorf, to a primitive or historical community of possession (*communio primaeva*), but it is an idea of practical reason (*communio originaria*) (MM 6: 251; MM 6: 258; MM 6: 262). It is an idea which can be neither proven nor disproven by experience, but which possesses a rightfully practical reality and which must be adopted if we are to gain a systematic knowledge of natural right (O'Neill 2015: 180, 190). More particularly, the Kantian idea of the 'original possession in common of the earth' is called to·play two key roles. In the sections dealing with property right, it appears above all as a precondition of the property of things, and ultimately of the property of land, the latter being the basis of any property of things. As Kant puts it,

> [T]his possession in common is the only condition under which it is possible for me to exclude every other possessor from the private use of a thing . . . since, unless such a possession in common is assumed, it is inconceivable how I, who am not in possession of the thing, could still be wronged by others who are in possession of it and are using it. (MM 6: 261)

Starting from the basic consideration that not all acquisitions of the external reality can be derived, Kant affirms that there must be some *original* acquisition and that such an acquisition can only proceed from a unilateral will since if it proceeded from a contract (and hence from what belongs to another), it could not be original but would be derived (MM 6: 266). Yet, as we have already seen, a unilateral will cannot impose on others an obligation that they would other-wise not have. Others can be obliged to refrain from using a given external object only through a will that is a common will, and hence only if they can

---

[23] Conversely, the reason why the issue of global inequalities is addressed here only through the lens of transnational migration and trade is that Kant's concern about inequalities at the domestic level translates into the recognition of a principle of formal equality of opportunity and that, in the global justice literature, this principle is typically invoked to defend the transnational mobility of persons and goods.

oblige themselves or exclude themselves from the use of that object. It is at this level that the idea of the original contract comes into the picture. No real contract is required before being authorized to exclude others from the use of an external object, otherwise acquisition would be derived.[24] But a contract is required as the focal point with which any external possession must accord (MM 6: 264). As Kant puts it, 'this requires a will that is *omnilateral*, that is united not contingently but a priori and therefore necessarily, and because of this is the only will that is lawgiving' (MM 6: 263). To this must be added that others cannot oblige or exclude themselves from a given external object unless they already possess it in one way or another (Chauvier 1996: 103–8). 'By my unilateral choice I cannot bind another to refrain from using a thing, an obligation he would not otherwise have; hence I can do this only through the united choice of all who possess it in common' (MM 6: 261). It thus appears that the idea of the original contract and the idea of the original possession in common of the earth work in tandem and together constitute the precondition of the property of a piece of land, and in a derivative way, of the property of things. A final point to bear in mind is that this community of possession must extend to all inhabitants of the earth since, given that the earth has a finite surface, it is ultimately all inhabitants of the earth who are likely to be affected by a property claim on a piece of land and who are expected to exclude themselves from its use. In Kant's words, an original acquisition of what is external 'will always remain only provisional unless this contract extends to the entire human race' (MM 6: 266).

This leads us to the second role played by the idea of the 'original possession in common of the earth', which dominates the sections devoted to cosmopolitan right and which is to ground the '*right of visit*' that is possessed by all human beings (TPP 8: 358). The original possession in common of the earth here no longer refers to a rightful community of possession (*communio*) but to the possibility of reciprocal physical action (*commercium*) (MM 6: 352). Kant tells us in this context that 'prior to any act of choice that establishes a right' – which means before any acquisition, and hence in an innate way – all human beings are in a possession of land that is at the same time *in conformity with right* and *common* (MM 6: 262). It is in conformity with right in the sense that all human beings 'have a right to be wherever nature or chance

---

[24] On this point, Kant departs from Pufendorf who, although also denying that a simple corporeal act (such as the fact of seizing an external object) could generate an obligation for another, concludes the existence of an actual tacit contract between people, according to which once a person seizes a common thing to use it, others may not take it from them. See: Pufendorf ([1672] 1729: vol. 1, book IV, ch. IV).

(apart from their will) has placed them' (MM 6: 262). They all have an innate right to occupy 'a' place on the surface of the earth or to be 'somewhere', and nobody has originally more than another the right to occupy a given portion of the surface of the earth (TPP 8: 358). It is common because the earth has a spherical form and its inhabitants cannot as a result disperse endlessly, but must inevitably come into community with each other. Whether they want it or not, all inhabitants of the earth are interwoven in a global network of reciprocal external actions that affect both their living conditions and their rights. And for Kant, who says inevitability of reciprocal external actions also says moral duty to enter a rightful condition: '(If you cannot help associating with other), *enter into a society with them in which each can keep what is his (suum cuique tribue)*' (MM 6: 237). This, as we have seen, is the substance of the postulate of public right. In this specific case, it entails that, since the inhabitants of the earth cannot avoid coming into contact with each other, they must subject themselves to a cosmopolitan right understood as a right 'necessary for the sake of any public rights of human beings' (TPP 8: 360) or as a 'rational idea of a *peaceful*, even if not friendly, thoroughgoing community of all nations on the earth that can come into relations affecting one another' (MM 6: 352).

From the 'right of possession in common of the earth's surface', Kant also deduces a '*right to visit*' or a right 'to present oneself to society' (TPP 8: 358). This right to visit or to hospitality plays an important role in the realization of cosmopolitan right. By allowing inhabitants of the earth to concretely and peacefully enter into relation with one another, it also allows the gradual implementation of public laws governing their possible commerce and hence the implementation of a cosmopolitan rightful condition (TPP 8: 358). However, the right to visit can also prove dangerous as its exercise can give rise and even be invoked to legitimize different forms of right violations. Just think, in this regard, of the way in which the ideas of original community of possession and of universal society of mankind invoked by thinkers such as Francisco de Vitoria, Hugo Grotius, or John Locke have been reappropriated in the course of history to justify practices of colonization. The risk of such abuses certainly explains the restrictive tone taken by the third definitive article for perpetual peace: 'Cosmopolitan right shall be limited to conditions of universal *hospitality*' (TPP 8: 357). Cosmopolitan right does not aim to promote the unhampered mobility of persons, but to strike an appropriate balance between the respective rights of global actors – such as individuals, tribes, commercial societies, and states – as 'citizens of the world'. This search for a balance reflects the irreducibility of each sphere of public right. The freedom of movement of individuals ought to be secured, but not at the expense of the capacity of states and tribes to determine themselves (Muthu 2012; Muthu 2014; Kleingeld

2013: 76, 138–9, 147).[25] The latter have the right to restrict access to their territory when they deem it necessary to prevent important injustices such as slavery, land dispossession, famine, oppression and internal conflicts (TPP 8: 358–9).

This explains Kant's claim that settlements on the territory of another state or tribe cannot take place without the agreement of the natives, but require a 'special beneficent pact' (TPP 8: 358). Even the right to visit is strikingly modest: although Kant talks of a 'right to visit all regions of the earth' (MM 6: 352) and 'to make use of the right to the *earth's surface*, which belongs to the human race in common' (TPP 8: 358), he also specifies that the right of foreigners does not extend beyond a right '*to try to* establish community with all' and that it is restricted to 'the conditions which make it possible to *seek* commerce with the old inhabitants' (TPP 8: 358; MM 6: 354). Put differently, the Kantian right to visit allows an individual *to try* to enter into relation with foreigners without being treated as an enemy (without being enslaved, plundered, or imprisoned, for instance), but it offers *no guarantee* of real visit – at least not if turning this individual away can be done 'without destroying him' (TPP 8: 358). We will return to this exception later.

Restrictions also apply to transnational trade relations. Even if Kant has an overall positive attitude toward trade, he is not an unconditional advocate of free trade and does not endorse the idea that justice requires the elimination of all trade barriers. This is evidenced by his explicit recognition, in *On the common saying*, that 'certain restrictions on imports' may be appropriate 'so that the means of acquiring livelihood will promote the subjects' interests and not the advantage of foreigners or encouragement of others' industry' (TP 8: 299). Kant's discussion of the permissibility of import restrictions illustrates an idea that we have already encountered in the previous section: states may in certain circumstances legislate with a view to the prosperity of their people, namely when they deem it necessary for the preservation of the commonwealth. A defence of protectionist measures is also found in *Toward perpetual peace*. After denouncing the 'inhospitable behavior' and the 'injustice' demonstrated by European commercial states toward those foreign peoples they have reduced to slavery or deprived of their lands, Kant approves the decision 'wisely' made by China to allow only access but no entry to foreigners, and by Japan to allow access to only one European people, the Dutch, while excluding it from any community with the natives (TPP 8: 359)

---

25 Kant recognizes that even if tribes have no domestic rightful condition (this is what distinguishes them from states), every people possesses an original right to unite itself into a commonwealth, which must be respected by other global actors (MM 6: 349).

By explicitly recognizing the right of states to refuse access to their territory to some types of imports, Kant runs counter to a particular interpretation of the principle of formal equality of opportunity, which demands the elimination of trade barriers on the ground that these barriers prevent some economic agents from benefiting from international trade in an arbitrary way, that is, because of factors that have nothing to do with their efficiency in the production of given goods and services. This version of the principle of formal equality of opportunity has essentially been invoked to denounce the fact that developing countries encounter obstacles when trying to export their agricultural and manufactured products to developed countries, while labour-intensive activities are activities in which they enjoy a comparative advantage (e.g., World Bank 2005: 208; Moellendorf 2009: 100; Tesón 2012).

We might be tempted to draw an analogy between this version of the principle of formal equality of opportunity and the one Kant endorses in the domestic sphere, and to argue that just as subjects should not be prevented from attaining a higher office or civil independence because of arbitrary formal barriers related to their social origin, so foreign providers of goods and services should not be prevented from enhancing their living conditions and thereby getting their country out of absolute poverty because of arbitrary formal barriers related to their country of origin. Yet, Kant introduces an important qualification when he grants states the right to erect trade barriers if they deem this necessary to avoid grave injustices on their territory. Even if he does not deny the benefits of international trade in terms of economic gains and even in terms of the development of global peaceful (i.e., rightful) relations (TPP 8: 358; TPP 8: 364; TPP 8: 368), through his theory of cosmopolitan right, he also invites us to consider the negative effects that international trade can have in terms of right. The end does not justify the means: neither the improvement of the well-being of mankind nor even the establishment of a rightful condition may justify the commission of actions that are incompatible with right.[26]

Even if international trade is today very different from what it was at the end of the eighteenth century, Kant's warnings remain of great relevance. Slavery does still exist in several parts of the world and cannot be detached from global production and distribution networks involving transnational firms and the Western markets they supply (Taylor and Rioux 2017: ch. 9). The economic activity of transnational firms also raises issues related to the right of foreign

---

[26] This is well illustrated by Kant's condemnation of colonization, which makes it clear that force or fraud should not in any circumstances be used to acquire the land of native peoples, not even if this would make it possible for them to enter a rightful condition, because we cannot 'sanction any means to good ends' (MM 6: 266).

peoples to their land. Consider, for example, the pollution caused by the release of toxic chemicals, the overexploitation of mineral resources, deforestation in favour of intensive crops, or the expropriation of local communities. It is also not unusual for industrial projects to face local oppositions and to end up in violence, sometimes perpetrated by the state itself. While Kant's theory of cosmopolitan right requires us to protect individuals' innate right to try to engage in transnational trade relations with each other, it also invites us to consider another aspect of transnational trade relations. Certainly, trade liberalization can be an effective means of promoting the aggregate economic growth of states and thereby of improving their socioeconomic situation. But correlatively, it can also weaken the position of states in the face of the growing power of capital. By allowing firms to relocate and/or subcontract their activities to places where labour and tax conditions are most favourable, free trade agreements can and have contributed to creating a competition between states in order to attract or keep capital, and thereby, to eroding their political autonomy in matters of labour, taxation, and wealth redistribution (Dietsch 2015; Ronzoni 2016).

Kant's theory of cosmopolitan right enjoins us to plug the legal loopholes left by existing domestic and international public laws, and to implement judicial mechanisms allowing agents affected by the activities of transnational firms to secure their rights. It also enjoins us to recognize that international trade laws that prevent states, and indirectly their individual members, from choosing their own domestic policies could not possibly be consented to by 'citizens of the world' taken as a whole, since states are not morally authorized to renounce their innate right to political independence and hence their capacity to determine themselves. This points to an important difference between the global and the domestic cases: while the abolition of barriers to the social mobility of subjects within a state is called for by the attribute of civil equality, the abolition of barriers to the transnational mobility of goods, services, capital, and economic agents appears as a possible threat for the independence and equality of states as well as for their capacity to address the wrongs committed on their territory. It remains an open question what the rights and duties of states are when no wrongs, but rather reduction in global absolute poverty or even republicanization of existing states, are to be expected from a removal of trade barriers. The logic underlying Kant's domestic principle of formal equality of opportunity might then perhaps justify a duty of right to liberalize trade. But in the current state of affairs, transnational mobility differs from social mobility in that it may not only lead to the commission of wrongs, but also undermine existing rightful conditions and hence the possibility of rightfully addressing these wrongs.

Let us now turn more closely to the transnational mobility of persons. Although Kant's theory of cosmopolitan right seems mainly to set limits to the free movement of persons, the direction and the nature taken by migration movements over the last decades may well justify a reversal of perspective. While the migrations targeted by Kant crystallize around the activity of 'civilized, especially commercial, states in our part of the world' (TPP 8: 358) and their 'trading companies' (TPP 8: 359) on foreign territory, those of greatest concern today are undertaken by individuals fleeing poor countries and looking for decent living conditions in another state, ideally a stable and prosperous state. Contemporary migrations have various causes, but several of them can be grouped under what may be called the 'increasing scarcity of inhabitable land'. Many population displacements are the result of internal conflicts (often fuelled by external armed interventions) that have devastated a region and made life miserable and uncertain in it. They are also increasingly caused by environmental damages such as hurricanes, floods, or desertification which, according to recent studies, are attributable to climate change and are predicted to multiply in the future.

Given the magnitude of this kind of migration, the limit that Kant explicitly places on the right of states to refuse a foreign visitor – namely, that this refusal may not involve their destruction (*Untergang*) – may turn out to be of major significance (TPP 8: 358). It may indeed mean that a considerable part of current migrants, and more specifically, those who have arrived on foreign territory and whose life would be threatened if they were turned back, have a special status and ought to be admitted as long as this admission proves necessary to their survival. This limit could be accounted for by the special physical relation that develops between the state and the needy foreigner arrived on its territory. By turning that person back, the state would not only fail to help them, but would also be actively involved in endangering their life. From this perspective, the duty of non-refoulement appears as a duty *not to wrong anyone*. But a useful insight is also provided by the idea of the original possession in common of the earth. If the 'increasing scarcity of inhabitable land' cannot be detached from a global network of complex relationships in which all inhabitants of the planet are in one way or another implicated, the admission of migrants on foreign territory may also present itself as a duty of rectificatory justice. As Kant indicates, 'the (narrower or wider) community of the nations of the earth has now gone so far that a violation of right on *one* place of the earth is felt in *all*' (TPP 8: 360). The interdependence that characterizes our world no longer allows us to absolve ourselves of any responsibility for right violations taking place on the other side of the planet. The admission of migrants would be a way to compensate for the 'increasing scarcity of inhabitable land' and for the resulting right violations, in which we are all irremediably involved. If we further bring into play the idea of the original contract, the admission of migrants on foreign territory may also turn out to be a duty of distributive justice. We have seen that a distribution of territorial rights cannot be considered conform to right if it is impossible for the whole society of states to consent to it. But there is no reason to limit the scope of the required 'possible consent' to states. As Kant's theory of cosmopolitan right points out, the scope of justification must also extend to all non-state actors that can be affected by a given distribution of territorial rights. Or as Korsgaard puts it, 'whenever we claim a right, we presuppose the organization of the whole human race into an organized body dedicated to upholding and protecting the rights of everyone, and commit ourselves to membership in that group' (Korsgaard 2018: 37). In the specific case of individuals fleeing their states because of an 'increasing scarcity of inhabitable land', the question to be asked is whether these individuals could possibly consent to a distribution of territorial rights that excludes them from any inhabitable land. And it is quite easy to see that they could not since this would amount to renouncing their innate right to freedom, which cannot possibly be exercised without the resources needed to live. If so, public laws authorizing states not to admit such migrants on their territory can hardly be considered in conformity with right, but ought to be reformed so as to ensure that no inhabitant of the earth is denied access to inhabitable land.

To come back to our initial question, namely, whether the duty to enter a rightful condition beyond the state also involves duties of right to combat certain forms of global poverty and inequality, the answer is thus partly positive. There are good reasons to think that rich states have a duty of right to assist states lacking the resources to fulfil the core functions of the state. Nothing stands in the way of extending the requirements of self-preservation and fair return from the domestic sphere to the global sphere. It can even be assumed that a society of states could not possibly consent to international public laws allowing some of them to flourish while leaving others unable to maintain themselves. Yet the same does not apply to the principle of formal equality of opportunity. Concerned with avoiding that the transnational mobility of goods and persons undermines the independence and equality of states, Kant grants states the right to refuse foreign visitors on their territory. An exception should, however, be made: this refusal may not threaten their lives. Certainly, there is still no talk of equality of opportunity between members of different states; but given the 'increasing scarcity of inhabitable land', this exception may nonetheless be expected to have important implications in terms of individuals' right to freedom of movement across borders.

5 Conclusion

This Element started by arguing that even if the Kantian conception of the duty of beneficence offers important conceptual and normative resources to address the question of global poverty, it also involves important limitations. As a conclusion, it may be instructive to return to these limitations and to examine to what extent the Kantian conception of global distributive justice, as we have reconstructed it, is capable of overcoming them. Let us start with the double limitation related to the wideness of the duty of beneficence. This wideness, and more particularly, the fact that the duty of beneficence implies the adoption of a principle of action rather than the performance of specific actions, seems to imply that a person could adequately fulfil their duty of beneficence without ever taking concrete action in favour of the global poor. Correlatively, by focusing on the positive respect that is owed to the rational nature of each human being, the Kantian conception of the duty of beneficence seems unable to account for the normative priority that should be given to situations of urgency that leave little or even no latitude for free choice. The recognition of a duty of right to assist those states that are unable to maintain themselves makes it possible to address these shortcomings. It must indeed be noted that this duty cannot possibly be fulfilled without concrete action being taken in favour of poor states, since it specifically requires working toward the reform of existing international public laws and implementing an interstate system of wealth redistribution in favour of those states that are unable to fulfil the core functions of a state. This duty can also account for the urgency of certain situations since it does not require rich states to help other states achieve their purposes regardless of their socioeconomic situation, but only to provide them with the resources they need to secure the lives and freedom of their individual members. To put it in terms of the idea of the original contract, existing international public laws ought to be reformed so as not to contradict the capacity of states to determine themselves, not so as to promote it. This does not mean that it would be contrary to right to reduce socioeconomic inequalities between viable states, but rather that it would not be contrary to right not to do so.

The answer to be given to the second limitation of the Kantian conception of the duty of beneficence, namely its non-enforceability, is more nuanced. Even if Kant emphasizes, first, that the global sphere is not only a matter of philanthropy or ethics, but also of right, and second, that right, unlike ethics, is connected to the authorization to coerce, he is more reluctant to allow the use of force in the global sphere because this risks undermining existing domestic rightful conditions and hence leading to a decline in terms of right. Still, this reluctance should not obscure the fact that duties of right, unlike the duty of beneficence, are duties that can be given by external laws and that external laws can and have been established in the global sphere in the absence of a global coercive power. There are even good reasons to think that these laws oblige global actors even if they cannot be enforced in practice by a superior power. This is what follows from Kant's recognition that it is possible for states to have 'provisional rights'. The notion of provisional rights indeed suggests that even before entering a rightful condition, states can have provisional territorial rights provided, first, they respect the existing distribution of territorial rights, and second, they are committed to reforming this distribution so as to bring it into conformity with the idea of the original contract – which, as we have seen, implies working toward the implementation of an interstate system of wealth redistribution in favour of those states that are unable to maintain themselves.

At this point, however, the question of paternalism comes up again. As a reminder, one of the objections that was raised against enforcing the duty of beneficence was the risk of abuse and arbitrariness. Why should it be any different for the proposed duty of interstate aid? It must be conceded that so long as the fulfilment of this duty is left to the good will of rich states, the risk of interference in the internal affairs of poor states is particularly high. Since the very viability of some states is at stake, the level of dependence on foreign aid can only be acute. This risk could to some extent be mitigated by implementing an impersonal system of redistributive taxation. However, aside from questions of practical feasibility, the question would remain as to whether wealth transfers should be tied to conditionalities. This is due to the mixed nature of the duty under consideration: on the one hand, it is a duty of right and, as such, it seems to be simply 'owed' to poor states, with no strings attached; but on the other hand, it is a duty with a specific objective – namely, to ensure the viability of other states – and achieving this objective is a far more complex and demanding task than maintaining the existence of another individual. The challenge will be to see to it that the aid provided does not undermine the right to independence it is aimed at securing.

The third limitation of the Kantian conception of the duty of beneficence is that, because of the meritorious character it attributes to actions of beneficence, it has the effect of generating a status inequality between benefactors and recipients – an inequality that can never be completely removed because recipients will never be able to compensate for the temporal advantage enjoyed by benefactors, who were the first to practice beneficence. To present aid as a duty of right rather than as a duty of beneficence will undeniably have an impact on the way in which donors and recipients perceive themselves and each other. As a duty of right, the duty to help states that are unable to maintain themselves in no way obliges these states, but simply amounts to giving them what they are owed, and more particularly, to treating them as full members of the society of states, capable of consenting to the external laws that govern them. Correlatively, fulfilling this duty does not confer any merit on rich states, not even if this is done on a voluntary basis. The reason is that an interstate transfer of wealth cannot be regarded as an action of beneficence if it simply amounts to giving another state what it is owed.

This fits in with the fourth and last limitation of the Kantian conception of the duty of beneficence that we have identified: a transfer of wealth cannot be regarded as an action of beneficence if the very possession of this wealth results from the injustice of the government. In the global sphere, this injustice is not introduced by a government, but either by the very absence of certain public laws or by the presence of public laws that could not possibly be consented to by all those subject to them. Such laws include, for instance, international laws that enable some states to enrich themselves while leaving other states unable to fulfil the core functions of a state, immigration laws that exclude human beings from any inhabitable land, or trade laws that undermine the capacity of states to determine themselves or to secure the rights of their members. Admittedly, in his theory of cosmopolitan right, Kant insists more on the right of states to erect certain barriers to the transnational mobility of goods and persons than on any duty to remove such barriers. Still, even if he does not seem ready to adhere to contemporary conceptions of global equality of opportunity, he may be assumed to take a critical stance toward any global inequalities that coexist with or are sustained by the non-viability of certain states, significant losses of political autonomy, or the relegation of certain individuals to the margins of any inhabitable land. The existence of such inequalities raises questions of justice and, by the same token, challenges the virtuous character or the moral worth that may be attributed to existing global aid initiatives.

That said, it is important to see that even if a justice-based approach allows us to overcome some of the limitations inherent to a beneficence-based approach, it is not to be regarded as an *alternative* approach to poverty and inequality. These two approaches do not present themselves as approaches between which a choice must be made, but rather as *complementary* approaches, each offering a distinct reason for action and each having its own strengths and limitations. Thus, duties of right and the duty of beneficence all essentially require us to agree with humanity as an end in itself, but the former requires us more specifically not to contradict it (a negative agreement) whereas the latter requires us to promote it (a positive agreement) while making sure not to contradict it. It is also worth recalling the strengths of the Kantian conception of the duty of beneficence: it presents the provision of assistance to the needy as a moral duty whose scope has no principled geographical frontiers and which brings into relief the greatness of every human being, while respecting their right to freedom. These strengths make the duty of beneficence a necessary complement to duties of distributive justice. Those who are proper beneficiaries of the Kantian principle of wealth redistribution or of the Kantian principle of formal equality of opportunity – whether in the domestic or in the global sphere – can be said to be provided with an additional reason to be assisted and hence to have a stronger claim to be assisted than those who can only appeal to others' beneficence. But beside them, there will always be plenty of other people suffering from poverty or caught in asymmetrical power relations, but who do not qualify for tax-funded assistance by their state, who do not belong to a state that qualifies for tax-funded interstate assistance, and who cannot afford to emigrate. In virtue of their profound and inalterable identity as 'rational beings with needs, united by nature in one dwelling place so that they can help one another' (MM 6: 453), they remain however proper recipients of our duty of beneficence. It is indeed only by making their ends also our ends – that is, by not being indifferent to the furtherance of their ends – that we come to fully appreciate the absolute value of their humanity as an end in itself.

References

Arneson, Richard (1989) 'Equality and Equal Opportunity for Welfare'. *Philosophical Studies*, 56, 77–93.

Barry, Brian (1982) 'Humanity and Justice in Global Perspective'. *Nomos. Ethics, Economics, and the Law*, 24, 219–52.

Barry, Brian (1989) *Democracy, Power and Justice: Essays in Political Theory*. Oxford: Clarendon Press.

Blake, Michael (2001) 'Distributive Justice, State Coercion, and Autonomy'. *Philosophy & Public Affairs*, 30, 257–96.

Buchanan, Allen (1987) 'Justice and Charity'. *Ethics*, 97, 558–75.

Byrd, Sharon and Hruschka, Joachim (2010) *Kant's Doctrine of Right: A Commentary*. Cambridge: Cambridge University Press.

Byrd, Sharon (1995) 'The State as a 'Moral Person'. In Hoke Robinson (ed.), *Proceedings of the Eighth International Kant Congress* (Milwaukee: Marquette University Press), pp. 171–89.

Campbell, Tom D. (1974) 'Humanity before Justice'. *British Journal of Political Sciences*, 4, 1–16.

Carens, Joseph H. (1987) 'Aliens and Citizens: The Case for Open Borders'. *The Review of Politics*, 49, 251–73.

Chauvier, Stéphane (1996) *Du droit d'être étranger. Essai sur le concept kantien d'un droit cosmopolitique*. Paris: L'Harmattan.

Cohen, Gerald A. (1989) 'On the Currency of Egalitarian Justice'. *Ethics*, 99, 906–44.

Collingwood, Vivien (2003) 'Assistance with Fewer Strings Attached'. *Ethics & International Affairs*, 17, 55–67.

Dietsch, Peter (2015) *Catching Capital*. Oxford: Oxford University Press.

Dübgen, Franziska (2012) 'Africa Humiliated? Misrecognition in Development Aid'. *Res Publica*, 18, 65–77.

Dworkin, Ronald (2002) *Sovereign Virtue*. Cambridge, MA: Harvard University Press.

Flikschuh, Katrin (2000) *Kant and Modern Political Philosophy*. Cambridge: Cambridge University Press.

Fraser, Nancy (2010) 'Injustice at Intersecting Scales: On 'Social Exclusion' and the 'Global Poor'. *European Journal of Social Theory*, 13, 363–71.

Freeman, Samuel (2007) *Justice and the Social Contract. Essays on Rawlsian Political Philosophy*. Oxford: Oxford University Press.

Guyer, Paul (2000) *Kant on Freedom, Law, and Happiness*. Cambridge: Cambridge University Press.

Hasan, Rafeeq (2018a) 'Freedom and Poverty in the Kantian State'. *European Journal of Philosophy*, 26, 911–31.

Hasan, Rafeeq (2018b) 'The Provisionality of Property Rights in Kant's *Doctrine of Right'*. *Canadian Journal of Philosophy*, 48, 850–76.

Herman, Barbara (1984) 'Mutual Aid and Respect for Persons'. *Ethics*, 94, 577–602.

Hill, Thomas E. (2002) *Human Welfare and Moral Worth: Kantian Perspectives*. Oxford: Clarendon Press.

Holtman, Sarah (2004) 'Kantian Justice and Poverty Relief'. *Kant-Studien*, 95, 86–106.

Kant, Immanuel (1996) *Practical Philosophy*. Transl. and ed. by Mary J. Gregor, intr. By Allen Wood. Cambridge: Cambridge University Press.

Kaufman, Alexander (1999) *Welfare in the Kantian State*. New York: Oxford University Press.

Kleingeld, Pauline (2012) *Kant and Cosmopolitanism: The Philosophical Ideal of World Citizenship*. Cambridge: Cambridge University Press.

Korsgaard, Christine M. (1996) *Creating the Kingdom of Ends*. Cambridge: Cambridge University Press.

Korsgaard, Christine M. (2018) 'The Claims of Animals and the Needs of Strangers: Two Cases of Imperfect Right'. *Journal of Practical Ethics*, 6, 19–51.

Laberge, Pierre (1998) 'Kant on Justice and the Law of Nations'. In David Mapel and Terry Nardin (eds.), *International Society: Diverse Ethical Perspectives* (Princeton: Princeton University Press), pp. 82–102.

Mason, Andrew (2001) 'Equality of Opportunity, Old and New'. *Ethics*, 111, 760–81.

Miller, David (2012) 'Territorial Rights: Concept and Justification'. *Political Studies*, 60, 252–68.

Moellendorf, Darrel (2009) *Global Inequality Matters*. London: Palgrave Macmillan.

Muthu, Sankar (2012) 'Conquest, Commerce, and Cosmopolitanism in Enlightenment Political Thought'. In Sankar Muthu (ed.), *Empire and Modern Political Thought* (Cambridge: Cambridge University Press), pp. 199–231.

Muthu, Sankar (2014) 'Productive Resistance in Kant's Political Thought'. In Katrin Flikschuh and Lea Ypi (eds.), *Kant and Colonialism: Historical and Critical Perspectives* (Oxford: Oxford University Press), pp. 68–98.

Nagel, Thomas (2005) 'The Problem of Global Justice'. *Philosophy & Public Affairs*, 33, 113–47.

O'Neill, Onora (1989) 'Universal Laws and Ends-in-themselves'. *The Monist*, 72, 3, 341–61.

O'Neill, Onora (2000) *Bounds of Justice*. Cambridge: Cambridge University Press.

O'Neill, Onora (2015) *Constructing Authorities. Reason, Politics and Interpretation in Kant's Philosophy*. Cambridge: Cambridge University Press.

Pevnick, Ryan (2008) 'Political Coercion and the Scope of Distributive Justice'. *Political Studies*, 56, 399–413.

Pufendorf, Samuel ([1672] 1729) *Of the Law of Nature and Nations*. Trans. by Basil Kennett, notes by J. Barbeyrac. London: printed for J. Walthoe, R. Wilkin, J. and J. Bonwicke, S. Birt, T. Ward, and T. Osborne.

Rawls, John (2001) *Justice as fairness: a Restatement*. Cambridge, Mass.: Harvard University Press.

Reidy, David (2007) 'A Just Global Economy: in Defense of Rawls'. *The Journal of Ethics*, 11, 193–236.

Rawls, John (1999) *The Law of Peoples*. Cambridge (Mass.): Harvard University Press.

Ripstein, Arthur (2009) *Force and Freedom. Kant's Legal and Political Philosophy*. Cambridge, Mass. – London, England: Harvard University Press.

Roemer, John E. (1998) *Equality of Opportunity*. Cambridge, MA: Harvard University Press.

Ronzoni, Miriam (2016) 'Global Labour Injustice: a Critical Overview'. In Yossi Dahan, Hanna Lerner and Faina Milman-Sivan (eds.), *Global Justice and International Labour Rights* (Cambridge: Cambridge University Press), pp. 27–52.

Rosen, Allen D. (1993) *Kant's Theory of Justice*. Ithaca: Cornell University Press.

Sangiovanni, Andrea (2007) 'Global Justice, Reciprocity, and the State'. *Philosophy & Public Affairs*, 35, 319–44.

Simmons, John (2001) 'On the Territorial Rights of States'. *Noûs*, 35, 300–26.

Singer, Peter (1972) 'Famine, Affluence, and Morality'. *Philosophy & Public Affairs*, 1, 229–43.

Stilz, Annie (2009) 'Why Do States Have Territorial Rights'. *International Theory*, 1, 185–213.

Taylor, Marcus and Rioux, Sébastien (2017) *Global Labour Studies*. Cambridge: Polity Press.

Tesón, Fernando (2012) 'Why Free Trade is Required by Justice?'. *Social Philosophy & Policy*, 29, 126–53.

Varden, Helga (2006) 'Kant and Dependency Relations: Kant on the State's Right to Redistribute Resources to Protect the Rights of Dependents'. *Dialogue*, 45, 257–84.

Weinrib, Jacob (2008) 'Kant on Citizenship and Universal Independence'. *Australian Journal of Legal Philosophy*, 33, 1–25.

Williams, Howard (2010) 'Toward a Kantian Theory of International Distributive Justice'. *Kantian Review*, 15, 43–77.

Wood, Allen W. (2008) *Kantian Ethics*. Cambridge: Cambridge University Press.

World Bank (2005) *World Development Report 2006: Equity and Development*, available at www-wds.worldbank.org/servlet/WDSContentServer/WDSP/IB/2005/09/20/000112742_20050920110826/Rendered/PDF/322040World0Development0Report02006.pdf

Ypi, Lea (2014) 'A Permissive Theory of Territorial Rights'. *European Journal of Philosophy*, 22, 288–312.

Acknowledgements

I would like to thank Howard Williams and the anonymous referees for their very helpful comments and suggestions on earlier drafts of this Element. I would also like to thank the participants in the Section on 'Kant on Political Change: Global Challenges' (ECPR General Conference 2018, Hamburg) and in the Workshop on 'Private Property and Territorial Rights' (University of Bayreuth, 2017) for illuminating discussions. I am especially indebted to Sorin Baiasu, François Blais, Mehmet Ruhi Demiray, Macarena Marey, Alice Pinheiro Walla and Garrath Williams. While writing this Element, I was supported by the Fonds de Recherche du Québec – Société et culture (FRQSC, 2015-NP-183033), for which I am grateful

Cambridge Elements ≡

The Philosophy of Immanuel Kant

Desmond Hogan
Princeton University
Desmond Hogan joined the philosophy department at Princeton in 2004. His interests include Kant, Leibniz and German rationalism, early modern philosophy, and questions about causation and freedom. Recent work includes Kant on Foreknowledge of Contingent Truths, Res Philosophica 91 (1) (2014); 'Kant's Theory of Divine and Secondary Causation', in Brandon Look (ed.) Leibniz and Kant, Oxford University Press (forthcoming); 'Kant and the Character of Mathematical Inference', in Kant's Philosophy of Mathematics Vol. I, Carl Posy and Ofra Rechter (eds.), Cambridge University Press (forthcoming).

Howard Williams
University of Cardiff
Howard Williams was appointed Honorary Distinguished Professor at the Department of Politics and International Relations, University of Cardiff in 2014. He is also Emeritus Professor in Political Theory at the Department of International Politics, Aberystwyth University, a member of the Coleg Cymraeg Cenedlaethol (Welsh-language national college) and a Fellow of the Learned Society of Wales. He is the author of Marx (1980); Kant's Political Philosophy (1983); Concepts of Ideology (1988); International Relations in Political Theory (1992); Hegel, Heraclitus and Marx's Dialectic; International Relations and the Limits of Political Theory (1996); Kant's Critique of Hobbes: Sovereignty and Cosmopolitanism (2003), Kant and the End of War (2012) and is currently editor of the journal Kantian Review. He is writing a book on the Kantian Legacy in Political Philosophy for a new series edited by Paul Guyer.

Allen Wood
Indiana University
Allen Wood is Ward W. and Pricilla B. Woods Professor at Stanford University. He was a John S. Guggenheim Fellow at the Free University in Berlin, a national Endowment for the Humanities Fellow at the University of Bonn and Isaiah Berlin Visiting Professor at the University of Oxford. He is on the editorial board of eight philosophy journals, five book series and the Stanford Encyclopedia of Philosophy. Along with Paul Guyer, Professor Wood is co-editor of the Cambridge Edition of the Works of Immanuel Kant and translator of the Critique of Pure Reason. He is the author or editor of a number of other works, mainly on Kant, Hegel and Karl Marx. His most recently published book, Fichte's Ethical Thought, was published by Oxford University Press in 2016. Wood is a member of the American Academy of Arts and Sciences.

About the Series
This Cambridge Elements series provides an extensive overview of Kant's philosophy and its impact upon philosophy and philosophers. Distinguished Kant specialists will provide an up-to-date summary of the results of current research in their fields and give their own take on what they believe are the most significant debates influencing research, drawing original conclusions.

Cambridge Elements ☰

The Philosophy of Immanuel Kant

Printed in the United States
By Bookmasters